OLD PEOPLE

They Don't Get Old by Being Fools

by Coleman Taylor

To: David & Linda
Thank you for all your support!
Coleman Taylor

DORRANCE PUBLISHING CO., INC.
PITTSBURGH, PENNSYLVANIA 15222

The events, people, and places herein are depicted to the best recollection of the author, who assumes complete and sole responsibility for the accuracy of this narrative.

ISBN: 978-0-8059-7756-1

Printed in the United States of America

First Printing

For more information or to order additional books, please contact:
Dorrance Publishing Co., Inc.
701 Smithfield Street
Third Floor
Pittsburgh, Pennsylvania 15222
U.S.A.
1-800-788-7654
www.dorrancebookstore.com

Dedication

DEDICATED FIRST to honor God, and give Him thanks for the many blessings. Thank you, Mom, for your wisdom that goes beyond words. Thank you, Dad, looking down from heaven on your third son. To my brothers and sisters, who have given me encouragement by words and examples. Thank you to all the old people in Lexington, Tennessee, for the great show of bravery and the passing on of your strength. In deepest love and appreciation to my beautiful, loving, and caring wife, Sara, my soulmate. To my children, Lauren, Ashley, Emily, and Kristen—you bring me joy daily. I cherish each day that we grow old together.

Table Of Contents

Introduction vii

Chapter 1   *Old People Don't Get Old by Being Fools*.............. 1

Chapter 2   *Nothing Beats a Failure but a Trier* 8

Chapter 3   *Can't Never Could* *14*

Chapter 4   *Don't Forget Where You Came From* *22*

Chapter 5   *Hard Start* *29*

Chapter 6   *Flowers* *32*

Chapter 7   *You Reap What You Sow* *41*

Chapter 8   *We Make Appointments* *47*

Chapter 9   *God Makes Disappointments* *55*

Chapter 10   *Old People Do Get Old* *63*

Chapter 11   *What Are You Going to Do When You Get Old?* *80*

Closing   *Reflections* *89*

Introduction

AS I approach mid-life and reflect back on my upbringing, I wanted to share a glimpse of the heroes of my life — old people. The old people were just ordinary people with a unique gift to share with the younger generation. These men and women struggled with things I can only try to imagine today. The struggles of segregation, the struggles of education, and the struggles of trying to make a living in an unequal world are only a few. These pillars of my community never shared any negativity with the younger people. No complaining or excuses from their struggles were ever given to the younger generation. If a person wanted to make it in this life, they had to go out and do it. The older generation would pass on their life wisdom through sayings. One of the sayings they shared with me and others growing up was, "Old People Don't Get Old by Being Fools." The wisdom here is, life is already written; you just have to live it, respect it, and don't be a fool with it. And you can also grow old.

The reason the old people gave us sayings was that many did not have an education and could not write anything down, so it became an art, storytelling, and the way they told the sayings was as important as the saying itself.

The person sharing their experience would begin with a relaxed demeanor and posture. In their conversations, many of the old people would not look you in the eyes. They would look around and smile and use facial expressions to convey their story. Then, in the midst of their performance, at the most important part of a saying, the old person would straighten up their shoulders, and their gaze would become focused on you. Their eyes would look straight at you, there would be a little pause in the conversation, and then they would share their saying with you. Even if the meaning of the saying wasn't very powerful to you, you knew it was important to that person.

This book was written to chronicle the life of my mother, Georgia Taylor. She had a very unique set of cards dealt to her in life. She was born with white skin into black family, and fought from the day she was born to be accepted. She has fought the fight of having a disability, and a husband dealing with alcohol addictions. She has also been dealt another challenge: Alzheimer's disease.

This book is written around sayings the older people used when I was growing up. Each chapter is a different saying. As the story develops, it will intertwine the storylines of the sayings, my mom's life, and getting older. I might not mention everyone who made an impact on my life in this book, but there were many people who helped shape who I am today. There were school teachers, coaches, farmers, neighborhood elderly, church leaders, and church members. So, as you read this book, I hope I have made you proud.

Just remember, old people don't get old by being fools.

Honor your father and mother, so that you may live long in the land the Lord your God is giving you. (Exodus 20:12)

Chapter One
Old People Don't Get Old by Being Fools

GROWING UP in Lexington, Tennessee, in the sixties and seventies was a great time for a young boy like me. Things there always seemed so routine and flavorful; routine because there was only the same things to do, day in and day out; flavorful because of the way people were and their character. It appeared to me, as a young person, during this time, that the old people in this town looked out for you in so many ways. In my little part of the world we, my brothers and sisters, were always exposed, or introduced, to the many characters in our play of life. In our town we had the black part of town and the white part of town. By the time I was old enough to go to school, the schools were integrated. I had several influences in my life in the neighborhood and out of the neighborhood. The way the old people looked out for you was very unique. Many who had education tried to show you the value of it and those without, or not given the chance to get an education, tried to show you the value of their informal education. In my life I was more exposed to those who had no, or very little, formal education. My dad had a high school education, and went off to World War II in the forties. My mom had an eighth-grade education. She got married and started a family. My grandfather, George Parker, my mom's dad, had almost no education; he was a farmer. My grandmother, Louise Parker, had almost no education. The Parkers were sharecroppers. They worked for a farm owner and produced crops and livestock, with pay being some cash and some portion of the crops and livestock. It was a common form of employment for African Americans, back then Negroes, after the Civil War. This was hard work and rewarding work: up before the sun, and work till the sun ran you in for the day. The afternoon was canning and fixing things from work. My grandmother had an undying spirit of working and

1

not stopping. She was the backbone of the family.

On my dad's side, Grandmother Taylor died before I was born. I didn't have the chance to enjoy her life or what she might have passed on to the next generation. My grandfather on my dad's side, Samuel Taylor, was class in action. Papa is what we called him. He had a profound influence on our lives. Papa was a first generation freedman. He shared that so often with the children, but to a young child born free, I did not understand what he was saying. Papa was born in 1895. I remember always thinking, he's old. Papa was educated. I don't know where he received his education, whether it was formal or self-taught. Papa could read and write very well. He worked for a nearby town of Jackson utility company for thirty-one years. He started in 1927 and retired in 1958. He passed on the power of success and that *you can do whatever you want to do* attitude. He had such an influence because we lived together. It seemed so common then that a grandparent, or both grandparents, lived with one of their children.

Our little house on 208 Wilson Street was humble at best. We did not have lots of money, but we had lots of love. Our house had seven rooms. The living room was the place where most families tried to have a couch and chairs, and present the family's best possessions. For my family it was different. My dad worked in car repairs during the day, and his hobby, or business, was working on televisions and radios at night. He had ordered a course on how to become a repairman for electronics. During the time when televisions had tubes and stuff, he had an important job in our neighborhood. This interest of Dad's overflowed into our living room. We had repair kits, broken TVs and radios, books, and all sorts of testing equipment. So the typical living room for us was a mess. What I found funny was that Dad could fix any electronic problem except the Taylors'. We would have a large color TV—yes, color TV—broken, but have a black and white TV on top of it. Sometimes he would have the tri-level of TV: lower level broken, with a medium TV broken in the middle, and the a thirteen-inch TV on top that worked. I never had the guts to ask Dad why.

The next room, to the right of the living room, was the children's bedroom. Six children: two girls, Brenda and Margaret, and four boys, Robert, Lloyd, Al, and me. We had a set of twin beds for the girls. They had a nice headboard with a sliding-door cubby. There was a bunk bed, where I slept on the top and Lloyd slept on the bottom. Al would share the bed with Lloyd sometimes, or with me on the top bunk sometimes. Robert had a rollaway bed and would pull it out nightly, or sleep on the couch in the living room some nights, not a lot of space for six little Taylors.

There was an archway in the wall that led to our mom and dad's room. They had a full-size bed wood headboard, a dresser, and a smaller dresser with a sewing machine on it. Mom and Dad had a gas heater in their room. We were cramped for space, but we had a few of the modern-day appliances. On the opposite wall from the archway was a door that led to the kitchen. The kitchen was small, with cabinets from decades past, a one-bowl sink, an electric stove, and refrigerator. Somehow, we were able to slide a kitchen table into this room. This is where a lot of the family time took place. Mom was always in the kitchen, singing and humming in the morning, when you woke up. The smell of bacon, toast, and fried eggs filled the house daily. As youngsters, we floated into the kitchen each morning to get our daily dose of a yummy breakfast.

The bathroom was in the hallway, off the kitchen. It was tiny, yet the walls were able to hold the tub, toilet, and sink. On a good day, you could almost get undressed in the bathroom. Over the tub was a window. This window had a view of the back porch, which was added on after the original house was built.

The room of lost dreams was the next door down the hallway. It was a room that Dad had converted to an office, for fixing electronics. The first memories of this room were scary ones. It had open TVs and radios, broken tubes, and test equipment everywhere. Spider webs and cobwebs in the corners of the room led you to believe that something had happened and that you should leave in a hurry. It was the beginning of a business, the ending of a dream. It was fascinating and eerie at the same time.

Papa's room was the last room in the hallway. Centered in the middle of the hallway was the room that all the sisters and brothers used to sneak into. Papa had several nice things that, as a youngster, you only saw on television, like palm fronds sitting in the corner. Papa had a wood chiforobe where he kept his expensive suits and ties. He was retired, and daily he would dress in a three-piece suit and go to town. He was class in motion. He would have on his vest with the silk backing that shone like a moonbeam. Paisley silk ties and his vest complemented the suits nicely. The vest had pockets; that's where his timepiece would go; the chain through the buttonhole and the watch in the right-hand pocket of his vest. He would put on his fedora hat and grab his umbrella and head to town daily. This is where being retired and having some success would pay off on a daily basis. Papa would sit outside the Rexall store and talk with the other old people who had nowhere to go and nothing to do. They, the old men, would exchange stories and talk about politics and current events. Papa would buy his newspaper, the *Jackson Sun*, and then walk home in the afternoon. He would sit on the front porch and read. One thing that I enjoyed about Papa was that he kept records of things. As he would read, he would write in his journal the things that had happened that day.

I recently found that book when visiting my parents' house in 2003. This is a lost art. By reading this book, I was able to look into how Papa thought about things: what was important to him, the things he thought were important to write about. There were clippings of court verdicts pertaining to civil rights. There were dates when someone came to visit him. He included information about the weather on certain days. He would write down information on current events. He left a legacy of the cloth from which I was cut. It made me proud to see that this old man, first-generation freedman, knew the importance of sharing himself. Papa wasn't a saint. He had his faults. The children felt that his harshness bonded us closer together. We were united to defeat the cause of Papa. Looking back, it's not a fault of anyone; he was not taught to love, so he didn't. He was part of a generation in which showing your emotions was a weakness. Papa was strong.

Our neighborhood was as colorful as it gets. Moonshine was the drink of choice. This was an economic equalizer. When you are raised in this environment, you think it's just the way things are. And it was the way things were. My brothers and I would watch police raids on the bootleggers in the community. There were four bootleggers on our block. When business was good, it was really good. On Friday evenings we would see various people come to our side of town. The traffic increased on Friday. By Saturday, things were in full swing. As early as nine A.M. the drunks were loud and already sharing their drunken state with the neighborhood. For our house, it was okay. Mom did not drink and made it known that she did not want that stuff around her home, or her family. When the local person would get intoxicated and maybe out of line, my mom would just say to him, "You know I don't want that around my kids." That person would then seem to try to walk straighter and say, "Yes, ma'am." It was a power that she used over and over. The reason for this is that Mom would not judge them. She made it known that she was raising her children. In an odd way, the response of these men and women was affirmation that they also wanted the same for their families. The people we saw were fathers, mothers, and people who had jobs, who were somewhat leaders in the community. She would not let us make fun or disrespect them, even when it would have been easy for my brothers and me.

The funny thing is, I learned business by watching the events of my neighborhood. When times were slow, one of the four bootleggers would call and report the other. The police would come and raid the house of the bootlegger. Today, this is called closing down the competition. In our weekly newspaper, the *Lexington Progress*, you would see the evidence of the alcohol in a dry county. Our next-door neighbors were the Parkers. This is a common name in this town. Earnest Parker owned a body repair shop. Men would work there and make a living. My dad worked there from time to time. The Parkers had expendable cash. The Parkers' mom, three daughters, and one son would travel to Jackson every Saturday to shop. To us, they were rich. So I had the desire to have my own business one day. Dad would spend his Saturdays fixing TVs and radios, and would deliver them during the day and collect cash. Things were different then. Today, when your television is broken, you go to the local Wal-Mart and get a replacement. Besides, electronics have come a long way since forty years ago. The children of our family would try to make a dollar. My brother Robert had a paper route. He would collect his money and save. He was able to purchase things like a motorcycle, clothing, and trips to watch the St. Louis Cardinals play baseball. The younger brothers would run to the store for the ladies in the neighborhood. We would get to keep the change, maybe five or fifteen cents. I remember Papa would ask me to run to the local store to get him snuff. I would. It cost him twelve cents, and we would get to keep the change of three cents. You learned that it took lots of trips to the store to make a dollar. But every time he asked, I went. It was his way of teaching us economics.

In our neighborhood, there was a code of ethics with the old people. If I was out of line while at someone's home or in public, it was okay, and expected, that an old person would correct me, even to the point of spanking or calling my parents. You did not want that call to make it home. So looking back at this time of molding my siblings and me, it was a good childhood. The thing that stands out the most are the people who took an interest in me. They wanted me to do good. They wanted me to do more than they did. They, the old people, wanted to be part of something they could sit back and say, "I had a part in raising that boy."

Encouragement came from within the family. Mom, for me, was the greatest source of encouragement. She may not have been wise to the proper ways of the world, but she was wise beyond the little town of Lexington, population five thousand. She knew people and the depths of good and evil that lay within man. Mom knew that her children could turn out to be adults whom she would be proud to claim, or we could turn out to cause her shame. She never led me to believe that I had a special gift. She was real about life. She would say, "No one is better than you, and you're no better than anyone else; if you want something, work for it." These words have been spoken by very popular businessmen today, but I remember dear ol' Mom's version back then. Encouragement also came from people outside the home: Mr. Johnny Jones and Mrs. Maggie Jones. They had no children living with them when I was growing up. One of the dearest memories was from Mr. Johnny. He had gone grocery shopping and had returned home. I was outside playing in the front yard. I looked to see him unloading the groceries out of the backseat of his car. I ran down and asked, "Mr. Johnny, do you need some help taking your groceries in the house?" He agreed, and I helped get the groceries in the house. He asked me when my birthday was, and I told him. I did not think anything about his question. Old people always asked questions of young people. On my sixth birthday, Mr. Johnny called to me, in the front yard, and told me to come down to his house. I ran down. "Isn't this your birthday?" I said, "Yes, sir." I was expecting maybe a dime or a quarter. He pulled out a box that had a baseball in it. This may sound strange, but I remember that birthday better than any birthday ever. I was so excited, and thanked him and ran home to show Mom. I played with that ball until I lost it in very high weeds one day. This present from Mr. Johnny made me want to do more good things for people.

Chapter Two
Nothing Beats a Failure but a Trier

MY MOTHER shared this saying: *Nothing beats a failure but a trier*, many times in my life. When I look back to the root cause of this saying and why this was one of her favorites, I find that it applied to every aspect of her life. In this saying, you see two people; the failure and the trier, a person trying. The wisdom in this is that both people are active in their pursuit. The failure tried, but did not complete their task. The trier is a person who once adversity came, had to keep trying. The failure is an example of what not to do. The trier is an example of persistence, pursuit, analytical thinking, and just hard work.

Mom, Georgia Louise Parker, was born June 9, 1932 to George and Louise Parker. From the day she was born, there was rejection. Her parents were sharecroppers and were known to be Negro. Mom was born with straight platinum-blonde hair, called a towhead, with blue eyes and white skin. Her father claimed that this baby, my mom, was not his child. Granddaddy is what we called him, and he was always controversial. Mom was born to a large family. Anna Lee, Eva, Betty Lou, Mary, Tom, James, and Willie Lee were her brother and sisters. None of her brother or sisters had the same physical appearance. From her birth, she was placed in a position where she had to try.

While she was growing up and working on the farm, there were many interactions with white people. Grandmama, Louise Parker, would work in the homes of the white farm owners. She would cook and clean. Mom would go with her. These farm owners knew Mom and never treated her any differently because of her color. I remember Mom telling a story of being with Grandmama at work. The farm owner's wife had a visitor one day. The visitor asked, "Who's child was that in the next room?" The farm owner replied, "That's my nigger's girl." Mom heard the conversation and just went on about her way. These words were almost enough to keep a young farm girl from trying. During those times, there was not really much you could do when someone totally disrespected you. It was the way things were. Even when Mom recalled this story, it was not told in malice or used as an excuse. It was just factual. It was one of the things that had shaped her in the formative years. It was motivation for her to try her best with the cards she had been dealt.

After Grandmama finished her work for others, she would go back to her home and do the same: cook and clean. She would work in the garden and can food from her garden. She would milk the cows and gather the eggs from the henhouse. She would feed the pigs and wash clothes. She would have dinner ready when Granddaddy came in from the fields. The children would also help around the house with the chores—hard work, if you will. The children would gather water from the spring, chop wood, pick cotton, pick beans, and do whatever was needed. One true test of a trier is growing food on a farm: your results prove very evident.

Life on the farm was filled with joyous times also. There were times when the younger children would slide off and play in the gullies. They would climb trees, slide down gullies, and play in the woods. There would be interaction with other white children the same age. Some would be the children of the farm owner, and others were the children of the people who worked on the farm, who might be distant relatives of the farm owner. The children would play together and have a good time. Things were harmonious until someone new would join the group; then the white children were not allowed to play with the black children. It was okay to play some, but when the children were able to enjoy one another, then there would be a breakup. This breakup would come at the direction of an adult in the white family. The message would come through *out of the mouths of babes*. These children would meet in the fields with the black children, and the announcement would be made: "We can't play with you anymore. Mom or Dad said that we can't play with you because we can't play with niggers." The separation would last for a few days, then the children, just like any children, would forget and go back to playing together. They really had fun. They could go away from home for most of the day and parents did not worry. The crime rate was low because all the crimes were committed at home: the bootlegging, fighting, and all that stuff. No one worried about kidnapping, murder, or rape. The children had acres and acres on which to play.

When I started work at the retail store, there was a lady who had grown up with my mom. I had never really thought about Mom's having white friends. When I talked to this lady, I was amazed. She knew my aunts and uncles. She knew more things about them than I did. When I returned home from work, I told Mom about this lady. She knew exactly who I was talking about. She also had great stories about her family and her. Ironically, when Mom and her friend talked about the old days, it seemed that it was a golden time. There were no hurt feelings or anger from years past, just respect and admiration for each other. They both had accomplished much with the cards they were dealt; more evidence of a trier's spirit.

The same thing happened to Mom when she went to school. Back then school was held in the local church. You had to walk about five miles one way to get there. Mom went to school, and there met more trouble. She liked being in school and wanted to learn the basics of reading and writing. Mom tells the story that she would play with the girls in school. Everything was fine with the children. Schools back then were segregated: black children went to black schools, and white children went to white schools. Mom was black, but had white skin. The little girls would play and get along fine until someone new came to school. Children can be very mean and hurtful. The children would play with Mom, and then invite the new girl to come play along with the gang. When the timing was right, the children would tell Mom that she did not belong at that school, because she was white. Listening to Mom at seventy years old tell this story made her sad. The pain of being with her own people, black people, and not being accepted, lingered with Mom for many years. She said that after the showing out of her playmates, she would go and play in the dirt by herself. This playing became something she expected every time a new student came to school—still not enough to deter the trier.

One of the highlights of growing up on the farm was going to town. Mom and her family lived about eight miles outside of town.

Mom tells the story that Granddaddy, Grandmama, and all her brothers and sisters would load up the wagon and head to town. The drive was one of drinking and having a good time. James, one of my mother's half-brothers, said one day when they were riding into town, "I know one person that will go to heaven in this family, that will be Monk," my mother's nickname." The nickname Monk was given to Mom when she was born, when a person made the comment that she looked like a monkey. The nickname stuck. The reason James made this statement was that while all the brothers and sisters were drinking and getting drunk, Monk did not take a drop. I asked Mom why she did not take a drink. Her reply was that she knew if she had ever taken a drink, she would have been the worst drunk in the bunch. She knew that once she crossed the line of drinking, she would never come back.

This played out in some of her family members. One of the acts that I remember as a small boy was when James and Granddaddy got into one of their drunken fights. This was common on the farm. Every time these two would get drunk together, the same fight would occur. It was because that James was not Granddaddy's child. He was born to Grandmama, and his father was a Pearson. The spirits would kick in and the topper would be the fight. This time the fight escalated to the point where my granddaddy had picked up an ax and was going to hit James with it. This would have caused death or very serious injury. Grandmama would always be brave. She stepped in between the two of them, and the ax handle came down. This blow hit Grandmama and broke both of her arms. One arm sustained a cut that needed stitches.

Mom must have seen events like this several times during her lifetime, only this time, a change had to be made. James was kicked out of the house and moved in with Grandmama's sister, Aunt Mary.

Mom met Dad on one of these trips to town. Mom's family came to town to get supplies needed for their household, and to partake in the festivities of the weekend. Some in the family would go to the courthouse and shoot marbles, some would go to the café and have a bite to eat, and some would go to the local bootlegger to meet with others to play high rollers. Gambling in Tennessee was illegal. The small-town gamblers would get involved in pool, craps, and cards. There was a lot of smoking and drinking that accompanied these events. So a trip to town would mean getting things like smokes, flour, sugar, and things that you did not have access to daily. In listening to the stories by Mom and Dad and other old people, it seems that town was like Hollywood, or New York City. Those who had a love interest would gather at the café. The café was part restaurant, part bar, part hair salon, part meeting room, and part dance floor, and even offered a little of the things that men were exposed to during the wars. Men and women would get dressed up and stay at the café for many hours. During the morning hours, it had a wholesome feel, where little boys and girls came to get a milkshake and a hamburger. The afternoon hours were filled with listening to a boxing match or sports on the black and white TV. The nights were more adult-oriented.

On one of these trips to town, Mom wanted to go somewhere in particular and was discussing how to get there with her sister Anna Lee. There was this young, strong, good-looking dark-skinned man leaning on a doorway. He spoke up and told the two sisters, "I'll drive there." My mom replied, "Oh no you won't." My dad knew what he was wanting to accomplish by this generous gesture, but my mom also knew what he wanted.

Mom and Dad started to see each other on a regular basis. Dad was living with another women at the time and had broken up with her. This lady was pregnant. The rumor was that it was Dad's child. Mom tells of the story that Dad took her to a house one day and they both went inside. As they entered the house, there were some older people who were sitting in the living room. Dad told Mom to stay here. She sat in the living room, and Dad went to the back of the house. He stayed back there for a long while; long enough that Mom yelled back, "Robert, I have to go." Dad came out of the back and they left the house. Mom asked Dad, "What were you doing back there?" Dad replied, "Fighting." The conversation took a turn about the lady's pregnancy. Mom told Dad that if the child was his, he needed to take care of it. Dad told Mom that this lady said the baby was not his.

Mom and Dad's relationship grew to a point where they wanted to get married. The new thing that was required for marriage was a blood test. Tennessee required this test also. The way to get around this little detail was to elope; that is what Mom and Dad did.

They went to Corinth, Mississippi, to get married, on April 1, 1951. They came back to Tennessee and started their new life as husband and wife. At this point, Dad had been living there by himself, and Mom moved in with him. Their new home had no wallpaper on the walls, just the bare necessities. Mom tells that the first night at her new home, Dad walked to the store and bought some bread and bologna for them to eat. Their love grew, and in the meantime, Papa was building a house across the street. This house was his retirement and where he would spend most of his time.

After Papa's new house was built, he moved there to live. Dad and Mom were invited to live with him. They took the offer. The house was a nice house, for the black neighborhood. It was a great change for Mom, who grew up on a farm, with the rarest of means. The new life was looking bright for the Taylors. On April 1, 1953, Brenda was born; in 1954, Robert was born; and in 1956, Margaret was born.

Mom, the trier, was in a place where her new life was getting ready to shine. It appeared that "the trier" attitude of Mom and Dad had succeeded.

Chapter 3
Can't Never Could

WHEN UNEXPECTED things come into your life, you have a choice to make: You can try or not try. The saying "can't never could" is looking at the word *can't* as a person. It is the attitude that lies within a person that makes them say "I can't," perhaps because of a life of failure, or maybe it's just easier to say "I can't." In reality, maybe you're choosing your destiny by the words you choose, I can or I can't.

Mom and Dad went to their bedroom to retire for the night (in 1959). Mom had always suffered from cramps in her legs. She would wake up from time to time and have knots in her calves. She would stretch and it would be better. On this date, October 24, 1959, Mom went to bed, as usual, and woke up paralyzed from mid-chest to the bottom of her toes. She could not move. She recalled waking up and telling Dad, "Robert, I can't move." Dad replied, "What do you mean, you can't move?" In both their disbelief, Dad laid mom on the floor by the bed, in the hope that it would help straighten out her back. After that did not happen, Dad called Dr. Raimer; this was back in the days when doctors made house calls. He came to the house and evaluated Mom, and he gave her a shot of muscle relaxer and told her that she would feel better in the morning. Dad and Mom went back to bed.

The next morning, nothing had changed from the previous night. Mom was crippled. Polio was common, and many thought it to be the common diagnosis for Mom. She was taken to a hospital in Memphis for more detailed evaluations and, hopefully, a cure. She was placed in a room and waited for the nurses and others to come examine her. When Mom's family came to the hospital, the hospital found out they had made a mistake: they had placed her on the *white* side of the hospital and had to remove her and place her on the *colored* side. I often wonder, if she would have stayed on the white side, would she be walking today? It's awful to think about, but true. It was later diagnosed that Mom had had a pinched nerve in her back, but the medical technology needed to help determine if Mom would walk was not advanced enough to locate the problem.

After getting some movement back, Mom went from a wheelchair to crutches to a walker. This took months. During her physical therapy, Mom was told that when she thought she could walk well enough, she could go home. They would schedule more therapy for her as an outpatient. When Mom got the hang of the walker the first time, she was gone—gone from the hospital, gone from the ties of doubt, gone back to take care of her family. Mom was put in a position where the word *can't* was not feasible to use.

The night that Mom became crippled was on their daughter Margaret's third birthday. Later Margaret said that for many years she thought it was because of her that Mom was crippled. This was not the case.

Mom shared how Dad had to take care of her, changing her soiled clothes, wiping her, and cleaning her. From the way Mom recounted this event, this might have been the first time that anyone had ever shown her any love—not the love that requires the feelgood stuff, but the love of doing the things you would do for someone else if they were in your shoes.

During this time, Mom tells of a small-town show of love. Dad had to return back to work at the block company, where cement blocks were made and trucked wherever needed. The first day back to work for Dad meant the first day for Mom to be at home with three children, trying to make it on her own. Dad left for work, but to Mom's surprise, he came back home. He was injured at work when a block fell on his foot, forcing him to go to the doctor; he was unable to go back to work. You can figure it out. This was a way for Dad to be home with Mom and take care of her. This was also a way for him to collect workers' compensation to help pay the bills. Even though my Dad did not say "I love you" much, every time I heard that story from Mom, it showed me how much he cared for her. Eventually, Mom started to get around and was able to do some chores in the house. Dad went back to work. Grandmama would visit and help with the house.

Mom and Dad's life got back to normal somewhat, with Dad working and Mom staying at home to raise her children. She would be there when children would come home from school. She learned to drive again. She would shop and do everything she did before, only with the addition of her walker. Mom and Dad decided to have more children. Their first attempt failed. Mom was pregnant with twins, but lost them prematurely. She carried them for six months. She did get a chance to see them and hold them, and named them Henrietta and Pencietta. Shortly after that, Mom and Dad were successful. They had a baby boy, and named him Lloyd Pince Taylor. Three years later there was another boy, Coleman David Taylor—me. Three years after that, there was another boy, Al Cory Taylor. There would have been more, but things in the house were heating up.

During the sixties and seventies, many families ventured into a two-income family. This would provide more income to do the things that your family always dreamed of doing, like having two cars, vacations, shopping, a better way of life with the things it could financially afford. For Mom, she wanted to go outside the house and help bring in income. Daddy did not want her to do so, and her new physical condition did not lend itself to doing so.

Mom was raising her six children, and did various jobs to help the family. She would sew for people in town. She was known to do alterations and to make clothes from scratch. She had a pretty good thing going. She would baby-sit children at the house. Dad would work and try to make a living working on cars during the day, and worked on televisions during the evening hours. His shop was our living room. We, the children, would play and just have a great time. Monopoly, snow cone, army men, Twister, cards, and Mystery Date were a few favorites we played, making for a fun and festive house. Boys soon started dropping by, trying to court the girls of the house. Things seemed to be back on track.

Dad would have a beer in the refrigerator. Mom and Dad would sit in the kitchen and talk for a while. Dad would have his beer in a brown paper bag. When one of the children would enter the room, Dad would hide the beer behind a radio or something he was working on in the kitchen. As children, we all saw it. We did not think anything about it. The neighborhood was filled with it, so no big deal. As the children grew older, Dad's drinking got worse.

Friday nights were the highlight for the Taylor children. Dad would come home from work and give Mom money. Two or three of us children would go with Mom to deposit some money in the bank, then went off to shop. We would shop at Big Star or Piggly-Wiggly. We would get our weekly supply of cereal, cookies, milk, bananas, hot dogs, and Cokes. Mom then would drive us home. The children would all come to the car and help put up the groceries, then Mom would boil hot dogs. We would each get one or two hot dogs and a sixteen-ounce Coke, and then go and sit in front of the television. *Hogan's Heroes*, *The Brady Bunch*, *Room 222*, and many more shows were the family's TV time. Saturdays were filled with running, from taking people here and there, to just getting things done. Once, every other week, on Saturday, my brothers and I had to go to the barber shop. This was a neat thing to do, but with afros and big hair, the Taylor boys were not in style. Saturday's dinner was the same each week: hamburgers and Coke. Boy, this was good! All the children enjoyed the weekends at our house.

As time went on, the drinking of alcohol became worse. Dad would not come home on Friday evening, nor give Mom his check. He started running with the boys, playing pool, gambling. Hanging out was his thing. When I was a child, seeing Dad come in late at night was common. Mom would still try to carry on with the children as normal. During the day Dad would come in and sit on his side of the bed. He smoked Salem cigarettes. He would fire one up, sit there, and then finally go to bed. Mom and Dad's bed was pushed against the wall. Dad slept in the front and Mom next to the wall. Arguments would start. The next day Mom would carry on as normal. One day, Dad came in late. All the children were in bed. Dad came into the children's room and demanded that Mom come to bed. She told him no, because Al was sick. He demanded again. Mom told Dad, "Robert, my baby is sick, and I'm going to stay in here because he needs me." Al was sleeping in Brenda's old bed. Brenda had moved away after high school graduation. Dad demanded again, "Georgia, get up and come to bed!" She started to answer, and then he punched Mom's stomach. It was quiet in the room and the blow sounded like an intense hit to Mom's stomach. All the children were in shock. Robert Jr. was at work, at the Dairy Queen; Margaret was crying; Al was too young to know what had happened; Lloyd lay quiet in his bed; and I sat up from the top bunk and try to comprehend what had happened. I wasn't angry. I was more concerned about Margaret and how she was crying. Dad went back to bed alone. Mom consoled us all while lying next to Al.

Dad would not be around on Saturdays. The repair work had stopped. The reminders were everywhere: broken TVs and radios were our decor. Dad would come in the late afternoon and lie in bed. He would not lie down head to toe, but across the bed.

Sundays we would go to church. In the afternoons we would spend time at Grandmama's or Aunt Mer's. Mom and the children did not think about the bad times; it was just the way things were. While visiting, we would have cousins and aunts and uncles come by and we would pass time enjoyably with family.

In the midst of all this was Papa. Papa made it known that the house we were living in was not ours, but his. He was the owner of the house. Mom could not do many things pertaining to decorations, or fixing the house. Papa did not like children very much. He was in a house with six children. He would correct us as we would run through the house. "Stop it, stop running through the house, you're going to tear it down." This was his retirement. For the children, we just wanted to have a good time. So every time a toy came into the house, he was on the rampage. Once, Mom had bought Al a beach ball and he was bouncing it, and Papa ranted, "You know you're going to tear down the house." Mom was so tired of hearing Papa talk to her children like that. Her husband did not defend them pertaining to the house issues. Mom was so upset that she got the ball and took a knife to it and threw it away.

Things for Mom were intense, always. She was discouraged from baby-sitting in the house by Papa. He was upset because it disturbed his sleep. Papa was paranoid that Mom was going to take over his house. Dad, during this time, had stopped working altogether. Mom had to resort to getting food stamps. I remember the talk in the car on the way to church. "I want you children to know that we have food stamps. I don't want you telling any of the neighbors about it." I remember being embarrassed by this conversation. I was probably nine years old.

Things kept getting worse. Dad was pulled over for DWI. He had to spend two days in jail. The pressure in the house was great.

Mondays were a battle while Dad was drinking. The children would get ready for school, and Mom would take us. If she could not, then she would call a neighbor to pick us up. Dad would be on the bed. If he had a job, he would have Mom call and tell the boss that he was sick and would not be in. Mom hated this part the most. She was not a person to lie. After the call to work, the arguments would start about responsibilities. One of the most unbelievable events took place when Mom wanted to fix up the inside of the house. She started to tear down some wallpaper. Dad did not say anything; he left. He went to a lawyer. He had a statement drawn up to let her know that it was his house and she did not have permission to make any changes. This resulted in Mom's being summoned to show up in court. During the court proceeding, the judge wanted to know why they were there. Dad stated that the house was his and that he wanted her to know that. Mom stated that she was trying to raise her children and wanted Dad to help. Papa was there and had to put his information into the fight. Papa asked if he could speak. The judge let him. He told about how Mom was baby-sitting for people during the day. He went on about how the house was his and he felt that she was taking it over.

After Papa finished, the judge took over. "You two men should be ashamed. This lady is trying to make a living and take care of her family. You're trying to tear her down. Sir," speaking to Papa, "why don't you want her to baby-sit?"

"It disturbs my sleep," he answered.

"What time do you get up?"

"About nine A.M., sir," Papa answered.

"You should be up at five and getting ready for the day. You should be applauding this lady for taking care of you and your son and the house."

The case was thrown out. He told Dad he needed to provide for his family. Mom did not want to bring this matter to the courtroom, but she could do battle when needed.

The house was not peaceful during this time. Dad was caught between trying to please his father, Papa, and trying to please his family. He was responsible for six children and for figuring out how to give them the things he wanted to give them. Dad had a faithful wife and wanted to help make a life for her, with all the added pressure of her life, dealing with being disabled. It finally resulted in another episode where violence had come into the house. Fortunately, Brenda was married now; Margaret was at church camp. My brothers and I were at Brenda's with her new husband, Jerry. The violence escalated to a physical attack on Mom, and Dad asking her to leave the house. She did. For Mom, can't never could. She had to succeed. No way to say she could not do anything. Mom had to learn to live again being disabled. She had to hold her head high when friends and curious strangers looked at her when she walked. She had to cope with people looking at her with her white skin while her children's skin was not. She had to learn to live alone again, without her husband.

Mom never looked at her disability as anything to hold her back. She found a house and moved out. With assistance from different agencies, and her extra odd jobs, she made it. For three years, we lived on the other side of town from Daddy. When you bottom out, you really bottom out. Dad started to drink more. We, the children, would see Dad from time to time in an embarrassing situation and would walk on by. That was not the man we knew growing up.

Then something happened to Dad. He stopped drinking alcohol. It told me that he decided he needed to make a change, and he did. He stopped cold, and never drank again. Later on he stopped smoking. Dad would visit from time to time with Mom at her new home across town. Mom would cook and feed Dad. They would talk for hours, and got to know each other again. The first Christmas we were away from Dad, he told Mom to bring us to his house on Christmas morning. He had three bikes: a ten-speed for Lloyd, and two three-speeds, for Al and me. This was exciting; however, Papa had to blow the excitement again. Al was visiting Dad a few days before Christmas, and Dad was not home. Papa, dressed in his daily suit, invited Al into the house. He said, "I want to show you something." He took Al though the house and showed him the three bikes. He wanted to make sure that we knew where the bikes came from; however, on Christmas morning, we were glad to have a bike, and thanked Dad. We rode our new bikes back to our home, across town.

For the children, we were happy. We had moved, and there was no extra TV equipment around. We could play and be kids without the yelling and hollering from Papa. We met new friends. We had a larger yard. We were free from the smoking, the drinking, and the fighting. We could be kids.

Chapter 4
Don't Forget Where You Came From

DON'T FORGET where you came from, because it is a shorter trip than when you left. This saying was shared with many people growing up. There were limited opportunities growing up in Lexington, Tennessee. Jobs were hard to find. Going to college was something only a few with wealth could afford. Those attending college were people with talent or those awarded scholarships. Back in the sixties and seventies you might have had relatives living in a larger city where you could go and live. While living there, you could search for a better-paying job and experience different things you didn't have back home.

Men and women also joined the military to go and see the world. At the end of their journey, they would wind up back home. Witnessing this, it became very evident what the old people were conveying. The sad truth of this adventure for these young men and women was that, in some cases, it did not give them any advantages over the ones who stayed and tried to make it at home. Many, upon visiting on vacation or on leave would return home. Many would return home happy to see friends and family. They would tell of their adventures. For a young person like me, I would fantasize about their adventures. I would add pictures to their stories in my head and try to imagine just how it would look if I were ever to visit such spots. As that person would brag some about their accomplishments, the old people would encourage them to keep going strong in their choice. It was as if the old people would get a little return on their investment when a young person would come home. The old people were proud of them and made them feel as if they were the most important thing while they were on their short stay.

After the college student or military person would leave from their visit, the old people would remind the ones in the house,

"Remember where you came from; it's a shorter trip back than when you left." It was a way to try to keep the local youth grounded. The old people wanted the young people to try to succeed, but to remain humble in their accomplishments.

Mom's way of showing us how to stay humble was in how she took care of her family. Mom showed this love for her family and fellow mankind in every way possible. There are several examples. Two Sundays each month, Mom would get her kids ready for church; and then she would take off and do her Sunday-morning routine. She would drive to pick up her Aunt Mary, Mer, as we called her; then she would go and pick up her mother and then head off to Sunday school and church. She would make the round trip without any hesitation. The trip one way was approximately fifteen miles. The reason for only twice per month was that the pastor had two churches, and our church had service on the first and third Sundays.

Sunday would consist of Mom's making toast, bacon, and scrambled eggs. The children would have gotten their clothes prepared the night before. So, after breakfast, we would get dressed. Dad did not attend church when we were smaller. There were some Sundays that I would have to get Dad to help me with my tie. He would sit at the kitchen table and drink coffee, while the rest of the house was in a flurry of activity. Dad would not discourage us, but he did not encourage us either about church. When all the family was ready, we would load up the car and head out to pick up the extended family. First, we would drive to Aunt Mer's. The funny thing about this trip was that Aunt Mer would call each morning precisely at eight A.M. My brothers and sisters always joked that if Aunt Mer ever died, we would know, because the phone would not ring at eight A.M. Aunt Mer would get in the front seat of the car with Mom and Lloyd; Al, and I were in the backseat. My sister Margaret would ride in the front seat, in the middle. Margaret would slide over and Aunt Mer would get in. We heard the same conversation that happened during the week when she called.

We would head off to Grandmama's. This became quite eventful. My Grandmama had the most beautiful white hair. She would cover it up with a wig. We did not know what to expect some Sundays. Grandmama would work during the week, cleaning homes for different people in town. They would donate to her some of their clothes, which were quite expensive. So Grandmama would come out with her wig and new, to her, clothes. The comments would come when Grandmama was coming out of the house. Sometimes the wig wasn't hitting quite right and Mom and Aunt Mer would try, in a nice way, to convince Grandmama that her own hair was more beautiful than any wig. This would sometimes heat up into a family quarrel, although most Sundays were very pleasant. Grandmama had a few adventures with her wig. One of the ladies got happy or shouted on Sunday. Some called shouting "getting the Holy Ghost." This would consist of the person screaming and repeating some praise while they would be out of control. To a young person viewing this, it appeared more like a person gone mad. This would usually happen around the climax of the sermon. It wouldn't be the same person each week, and sometimes no one would get happy or shout. Well, this one Sunday, Grandmama was by the lady who started shouting. The lady's hands and arms were going back and forward, clapping. As Grandmama went to fan this fellow sister, the lady's hand hit Grandmama in the head and her wig went flying. As dramatic as the shouting was, this was funny. I remember looking at Grandmama picking up her wig and sitting back down. Church was always exciting.

Mom must have had the patience of Job. She would handle life with six children and a husband trying to cope with the things that life had dealt him. Mom lived a full life, and there were things that always popped up from time to time, to keep it interesting. A typical Saturday would consist of having the chores broken down between the children: running to pick up Grandmama to bring her to town to shop, then getting things done. Her Saturday dinner was the same as long as I can remember. Friday night was grocery shopping, and then coming home to have hot dogs and Coke. Saturday ran from the sun up to sun down. As the children would start settling in Saturday night, it was very common for Granddaddy George to show up. He would be three-sheets-to-the-wind drunk. He was a happy drunk around the children. His favorite saying as he stumbled into the house was, "I love everybody." Then he would say, "Monk, could you drive me home?" She would. The younger children would ride along with Mom on the trip out to the farm. She was never upset or put out by this drunken weekly drive. Sometimes we would get home and settled and there would be another knock at the door. It would be Granddaddy again. How did he get back to town? This time he was more intoxicated than the first trip home. Mom would get up, get dressed, and drive Granddaddy home again. She never showed any anger while taking care of her family. On some Saturday nights she would have a visit by James, her half-brother, asking for a drive home. She would. Tom Parker was Mom's younger brother. Tom was a handsome man. Tom had dark, shiny, wavy hair. He had a bright, perfect smile. He was quiet and a hard worker. Women admired Tom, and he never let any woman get too close. I cannot remember a time when Tom had a girlfriend. He was always running with the boys. He was a man's man. Tom lived with Grandmama and Granddaddy. He and Granddaddy would work on the farm for the farm owner.

The house where my grandparents lived was a small place. It had a living room, a kitchen, and two bedrooms. It had an outhouse on the property that was later changed when the owner added another two rooms, converting one of the old bedrooms to a bathroom, in the seventies.

Growing up, my brothers and sister would love to go out to the farm to see our grandparents. There were acres and acres of land. We would go and fish in the one of the two ponds on the farm. There was a barn where the cows for the family were kept. There was a garden where my grandmother grew items to can and make food for the family. There were hills and hills of land. Cows would roam and eat in the pastures. The wind would blow and you could see God's hand moving the fields as the wheat would flow in an engaging pattern. Butterflies bounced from here and there. The children were just in such a safe environment. Looking back now, we could have been hurt by so many different things, but somehow, life on the farm was honored. There were the salt pits, for storing cured meats, and the hen house. There were apple trees, peach trees, blackberry bushes, grapes, watermelon, and all the fresh vegetables you wanted. My personal favorite was the fresh-picked corn on the cob. My brothers and sisters would get to experience different things, from growing up in town.

One experience that brings back a memory for me was the day

that Mom took my little brother Al and me to Grandmama's because they were killing chickens. If you have never seen this before, it can be disturbing. After raising your chickens, you would have a time set aside to process them for meat. This would consist of Grandmama and Mom going and getting the chicken by the neck and bringing it over to the stump by the woodpile. Then Grandmama would lay the chicken's neck on the stump, and with a hatchet, a small form of ax, would cut off the head of the chicken. The chicken would jump ten to twelve feet high, and this would go on for minutes. This day, Al and I were in the house watching through the window in the living room. We watched the first chicken go and were amazed. We wanted a closer look. We opened the door and watched another chicken go flopping around. I was still in amazement, but Al was not. He looked at me and said, "My stomach is getting sick." We went back into the house.

During these visits to the farm, we would unexpectedly meet cousins, aunts, and uncles who were also there to pay a visit to Grandmama and Granddaddy. We would play and get to know our family a little better. We would see Tom, but he did not make much conversation. He would sit in his bedroom and watch TV and have a beer. Tom liked to smoke. This was just one of the things that just about everyone at that time did. I remember, as a seven-year-old boy I would ask my uncles and Granddaddy if I could roll their cigarettes. They smoked Prince Albert in a can. My brother, cousin, and I would all take a turn rolling smokes.

As time went on, the farm remained the same. Tom stayed with my grandmother and grandfather. The cousins and families grew, and we would only visit a few times a year. At Christmas we would gather unprompted. Summer visits and a trip to see our grandparents seemed routine. Things were routine until Granddaddy got sick. He had a stroke on December 26, 1977. Granddaddy was paralyzed on his whole left side. This changed life at the farm. His career as a farmer was over. He couldn't do hard labor. After a few weeks in the hospital, Granddaddy was released to come home. He had a hospital bed in his room, and a portable potty that he had to learn to use. I had been a volunteer at the local hospital in the physical therapy department while in high school. I had started to work with Granddaddy on his range-of-motion exercises and walking him around the house. This aided him with adapting to home life. Granddaddy always had to do things his way. In his first few months home, he was tired of staying in the house. He wanted to visit friends. He started out of the house with his new walker and made it to the end of the driveway; this was about seventy-five yards from the house. As Grandmama returned back home, to her surprise, there was Granddaddy at the end of the driveway. The only problem was that he was tired, so Grandmama ran and got his wheelchair and brought it to him. This was a great show of determination, and also a great lesson in realization. It hurt my granddaddy that he wasn't the same man he used to be, because he had to learn to live again. As a man who was a gambler and a drinker, he had to learn that there was life without those vices. Looking back, it was pretty strange to see him sober. He had so many stories to tell. The stories were so funny and ironic about his drinking days. I got to see him not only laugh at himself, but also encourage his grandchildren to be better than he was. I would visit with him weekly the first few months and do his range-of-motion exercises until I felt that he was at a point where he was going to work at keeping his limbs loose. I would visit less and less because I was starting college. His present condition did not improve over the next ten years, and he surrendered to the truth and accepted Christ. His rebellious spirit became sweet as honey.

Grandmama remained the same during these years. She worked hard around the house and kept things going. She would cook and clean and do a little gardening. She worked some outside the house. Her main goal was Granddaddy. Her love for him was shown over and over again. She changed his soiled sheets, cleaned his portable potty, fed him, washed him, and cared for him. She cared for him better than any hospital or nursing home could.

Tom continued to work on the farm during this time, and still worked for the farm owners. He would stay in his room when most company came by to visit.

As a young person, viewing the changes in my grandparents, I realized that things don't remain the same. The memories of when I was eight years old had drastically changed when I was eighteen years old. The humble beginnings on the farm were great memories; then I realized that the farm was not owned by my grandparents. These great men and women had worked hard all their lives. What did they accomplish? What did they have to show for it? Will I be like them? These questions lingered in my mind as I was developing into a young man.

As I started my professional career, these truths were with me, and still are. I cannot forget where I came from, because the parents, grandparents, and old people had given what they had—their little wisdom. This wisdom, however, has played an important part of my "never say die" attitude in life.

They accomplished teaching their grandchildren that life is hard work, and that through hard work, you can have fun and provide your family a place to live. They had grandchildren attend and complete high school and college. They accomplished having grandchildren to do an honest day's work for an honest day's pay. They also taught their grandchildren that it's great to be yourself.

Will I be like them? You bet I will. I look back and realize that the things they endured were far greater than the things I face today. I will remain humble, because I might have to return one day to my beginnings and start over. Just remember, don't forget where you came from; it's a shorter trip than when you left.

Chapter Five
Hard Start

THE INFLUENCE of the old people around me in my formative years developed me. The strong teachings of my mom, teaching all of her children about Christ at a very early age; that I couldn't go anywhere that God didn't know what I was doing: This was probably the most effective discipline tool that was used to get me in line with what Mom wanted me to do. The old people had the same effect. As a young person, everywhere you looked there were old people. They were more intimidating than the police, and more comforting than my favorite blanket. This kind of love and discipline is what I missed most when I left for college. When I finally left home to go to college, I thought I could get away from this routine, boring life. I was right, but also so wrong. When I started college, I thought I was going to be something different from the other six thousand students at the University of Tennessee at Martin. I believed this was my big chance to hit it big. I believed that if I could be unique and stand out, somehow that would make me more marketable. I had no idea that schoolwork played a part in being successful. To make a long story short, I lost the old me, the person I was when surrounded by old people—the person I was proud of being was lost. At the end of getting my degree, I didn't care enough to go through the graduation ceremony. I was content knowing I had gotten a degree. What was my next step?

When I was in elementary school, I had a dream of becoming a physical therapist. I entered college with the hopes of obtaining this goal. As the influence of my upbringing changed, so did my goals. I finished college with a BS in communications. I thought I would be the next great TV personality on *Entertainment Tonight*, or MTV. That did not happen. I ended up not being able to find a job. The Catch-22 of the highly educated is, how to I get the job without experience? How do I get the experience without the job? I found the answer. Start with a step. I picked up a job at a local retail store. It was a large chain of stores. I started there by getting shopping carts off the lot and unloading trucks. I remember that I had worked several jobs to get my education, along with some grants, and loans; and now, after an expensive education, I can unload trucks.

This period of my life was the lowest of my existence. I applied for jobs in Memphis, Nashville, Jackson, and anywhere else I could send a resume. No one answered my mail. I thought I had a job with the Jackson television station WBBJ. It was a chance to do camera work. I was told I had the job. I filled out the paperwork, and was instructed that when it was returned from the main office in North Carolina, they would call and I would start work. Well, I was still working at the local retailer making some income. During this time, I felt God's pull on my life. Every billboard I read outside a church had a message for me: *God must melt you before he can mold you.* Years later, I can still see that billboard. The old people in the community knew I was struggling to get a start. It seemed they were well aware of the struggles, and had an saying for me: *Hard start means a good finish.* The wisdom in this is that if you are really trying, then the experience itself is valuable. I found out what I did not want to be, and grew stronger in my search. My search was in many areas. What did God want for me? What did I want to do? What was the limit I would put myself through to get started? Well, answers come in many different forms. I used to pray that God would give me the wisdom of Solomon, the strength of Samson, and the patience of Job. God answers prayers. When I shared this prayer with Mom, she laughed and said, "That's your problem. If you pray for patience, then God will put you through things to obtain patience. You should be praying for strength."

One day, when I was working at the retail store, I was called to perform a cleanup in ladies wear. I went with my mop and bucket. but to my surprise, it was an old friend and football mate. He had been married for a few weeks and his new bride was believed to be pregnant. On the floor was the result of that belief: turnip-green puke. I had the great joy of cleaning this up. As I stooped to clean it with a paper towel, the smell of this concoction hit my face and almost put me out for the count. My mouth was getting watery and my stomach was getting jumpy. I thought I might be adding to the up-chuck. As clear as if talking to a person in front of me, I said, "God, I'm through fighting with you. If this is what you want me to do for the rest of my life, I will do it. I'm tired, I'm tired."

I made it through the cleanup. I felt a release on my spirit. I had somehow made peace in my soul over this smelly mess. I had, at this point, been looking for a job for nine months. Things changed. I received a call from my brother in Orlando, Florida. It was the fastest-growing city in the United States during the late eighties. He advised me, "You can find a job here, and your chain of stores has a location only five miles away." I called the next day and received a transfer to a store in Casselberry. I started the move to Florida, and in five months, finally got that break into management. I was an assistant manager, earning a decent salary, which then opened more doors within the company. I finally received that call from WBBJ only six months later. I was then out of Tennessee and had my entry-level job with a great retailer. Hard start.

Chapter Six
Flowers

EVERY FIRST Sunday in May was Timberlake Grove Baptist Church's homecoming. This was a time when former members would return to see relatives at their home church. This was an exciting time for church members. A typical homecoming consisted of Sunday school in the morning, a church service that started in the morning and ended early that afternoon, dinner on the grounds, and then a second church service. Members dressed in their finest clothes, and invited others in the community to come by and join in the festivities.

Days before homecoming church service on Sunday, there was an appointed time that the family would go and clean the grave sites. Many who were returning for homecoming would go to the grave site and visit their loved ones. Mom, Grandmama, Aunt Mer, and the Taylor children would pile into one car. Each of the adults would bring gardening tools, a rake, a hoe, a lawnmower, and a sling blade. Each adult would have picked out artificial flowers during one of their trips to town and stored them away for this day to clean off the grave sites. Once we arrived at Kizer Cemetery, we would all go to work. We would rake and pull weeds, cut the grass, pick up fallen branches, and dig dirt to fill the sunken grave sites. Once the site was clean, the finishing touch was placing the artificial flowers on the site. Some graves had live rose bushes that bloomed each year.

As we would looked back at the sites, we could see the improvements made, and Mom would always comment about the flowers: "Those flowers look so pretty; I want you to give me my flowers while I'm living so I can enjoy them," she would say.

Flowers come in many different forms. They can be real flowers, good deeds, good works, a kind word, good friendship.

Another important part of cleaning the graveyard was learning about each grave site. We would look at the different names on the tombstones, and the adults would start telling the history of that person. They would tell you how they were related to someone who was living, or how they were related to you. It became a genealogy lesson at the graveyard. No one ever took the time to write this information down, but would share stories about each of the deceased. They would make a good comment, or say something funny about that person's character. For my great-grandfather on my mom's side—his nickname was Pap—Mom would comment about how Pap used to yell when he got drunk, and then the others would join in with their comments, and it would be a very pleasant, entertaining time at the graveyard.

The main event was Sunday dinner on the church grounds. Church members would cook several treats and bring them to share with visitors. There were some tables built several years ago and stationed behind the church. The ladies would roll out their red and white tablecloths over the tables and set out their fine china. A typical church family would bring fried chicken, turnip greens, potato salad, banana pudding, cake, and many other goodies. There would be a visiting church that would attend and conduct the afternoon service, so there was a certain amount of pride that went along with the size of the spread you laid out before your company. As children, my brothers and sisters would get in line and get some of every dish. Our plates were full to overflowing. We would take the plate of food back to the car and eat there. We would have to get Mom her plate, and Grandmama and Aunt Mer would make sure that Mom had been served. Mom could not stand in line to serve others for a long period of time, but she made her contributions by making dishes for the grand event. Pimento and cheese spread, homemade, of course, fried chicken, cakes, banana pudding, and drinks were a few things that Mom would bring to be part of the event. Many members would eat and go home and not stay for the second service of the day. For a child my age, this was bittersweet. I loved the dinner and the amount of food that we were able to get, but it was bitter because of the amount of time we had to spend at church. For my family, we started picking up Aunt Mer and Grandmama; then we went to the services for the day. We left home at nine-fifteen A.M. and returned again around five or six in the evening. The children were smart. We would sneak out of the second service and go play in the woods. While church was going on, we were out playing and trying to outdo the other children's lies. We would go exploring in the woods and sit in the car and talk. Sometimes we would go from one family's car to the other, just talking. When church was over, we went home. I never remember Mom getting upset about our not being at the second service.

After many of years of making that trip to pick up her mom and aunt, things changed some when Granddaddy had his stroke. He had gotten to a point where he could stay at home while Grandmama went to church. He had recuperated to a point where he could go from his bed to the living room. He could get into his bed and use the Porta-Potty if needed. So when Grandmama went to church, it was good on many different levels: Grandmama got a break from the daily caregiving role, and the children would pop in and say hello to Granddaddy. This seemed to cheer his spirits, and it was good seeing Granddaddy.

After being confined to the house for ten years, Granddaddy had grown old to the daily routine. He had told all his jokes, he had settled the question of where he would spend eternity, and he had told his old stories more than once. He decided that he did not want to live anymore. So later that week, he was in the hospital holding onto life. He had become ill and had to be hospitalized. I knew when he went in this time that it would be his last. Mom and Grandmama would spend the night with Granddaddy. They would lie in the chair beside his bed and make sure he was all right. They spent days in the hospital. Grandmama and Mom were worn out. They kept guard over Granddaddy day and night. I remember going out to the hospital on July second. Granddaddy was unconscious and could not speak. I remember that Mom and Grandmama were so worried. I glimpsed Granddaddy's legs and they were just moving. They were jumping up and down. Even the leg that had been paralyzed for ten years was moving up and down. I remember thinking, as I looked at Granddaddy, that he was getting ready to dance in heaven. I gave Grandmama and Mom each a hug and went home.

Mom recalls that a fellow church member, Mrs. Clara, had visited them. She left about midnight. Mom and Grandmama were tired.

Grandmama was to be asleep and Mom was to be on watch. Mom closed her eyes. She opened them to look at Granddaddy and saw his mouth move. Grandmama moved to his side. Mom stood up and stood by Grandmama. Mom said, "He's dying." Grandmama replied, "I know, he passing on." Granddaddy was asleep and slowly took his last breath. He was at peace. He was not in pain anymore and there was no more suffering.

About two in the morning, the phone rang and it was Mom. She was sobbing on the phone and asked me to come pick her up at the hospital. Mom stated that she could not drive. I remember that she knew early that evening that this was coming. Why was Mom so shook up? The answer is that her dad passed away. All of the family took it hard. Tom, the son that lived with Granddaddy, was so shook up that he could not take himself to the viewing or the funeral. He did as he always did: He sat back in his room and lived his quiet life. No one ever knew what, or how, Tom was thinking.

Mom gave her flower to the living in more ways. She gave what she had. Mom could drive and be there for you when you needed her. Tom, Mom's brother, was a hard-working farmer. Tom never married. He had started calling in to work sick on Mondays. It seemed to those in the family that Tom had lost his direction pertaining to work. Those around him thought that maybe drinking on the weekend had become more important than work. Tom stayed true to his convictions. He stated that something was wrong. He was throwing up blood on a regular basis. He finally went to the doctor, and they found there was a mass on his vocal cords. After many visits up and down the road to doctors, the decision was made to have surgery. Mom was always there to drive Grandmama and Tom to the doctors. Trips to Jackson were forty miles one way; trips to Memphis were one hundred ten miles one way. Mom would drive in the car we had. The cars we had over the years were always interesting at best. Some of the cars worked beautifully, and some not so well. The condition of the car did not matter to Mom. She was going to get you where you needed to go, no matter what. Somehow Mom thought that even through pure willpower, she was going to make it to her destination. And somehow she always did.

Over many trips, and a diagnosis of throat cancer for Tom, Mom started in and did what she did best: being a flower. Tom had a mass the size of a baseball in his throat. The doctors agreed that the only way to get the cancer was for him to have throat surgery and completely remove the tumor and also his vocal cords.

I remember living with Lloyd in Orlando, when Mom called the night before Tom's surgery. She told me that Tom would be admitted to the hospital and that his voice box would be removed. She wanted me to have a chance to talk to him and also a chance for me to hear him while he could talk. Tom and I had a five-minute conversation. Thinking about this was almost too much to bear, knowing that Tom's great smile and good looks would be overlooked by the hole in his throat and the inability to talk.

The surgery was believed to be a success. Tom returned home after a short hospital stay, and Mom and Grandmama were right there by his side. After a few follow-up visits with the doctor, the evidence of the surgery's success did not pass the test. The cancer was back and was spreading through Tom's body. After receiving a feeding tube and a trachea tube, he needed someone to help him get through this agony. There were also Tom's new looks. No women were coming around to see him, nor male friends; just Tom on his hospital bed, in his room. The same room where he had spent so much time had become his waiting cell for death. Grandmama and Mom gave him his daily medicines and talked to him through the use of pencil and paper. Mom tells of the trips to Memphis, taking Tom to the doctor, and how those times were often sweet. He would pass a paper with a question or joke on it, and they would have a good time going up and down those roads.

As the pain and failure of his body grew, the trips to Memphis became fewer, and the pain and suffering became more. Mom was there, right beside her brother, giving him food through his tube, giving him medicine. She would make the trip daily, sometimes more than once, to work with Tom, and to offer Grandmama her support. Mom led Tom to the Lord during this time and felt sure that he was serious and sure of his commitment to God. Tom died one year, one month, one week, and one day after Granddaddy. The house of three was now one.

During the time that Tom was going back and forth to the hospital for treatment, Grandmama was diagnosed with cancer too. Grandmama had always had a large midsection, as long as I can remember. Upon her visit to the doctor, she had to have surgery to remove a tumor. This tumor was on her stomach. She went in and had it removed. The doctor stated that the tumor was the size of a bowling ball. It's a wonder that Grandmama did not die first with that inside her.

My brother Lloyd and I were living in Orlando, Florida. We were both single and had jobs. When we got the news of Tom's passing away, we made plans to fly to Nashville and rent a car to make it home to Lexington. We made the proper arrangements at our respective jobs and made time to go pay our respects to our uncle. When we made it home, we saw our mom and dad and headed out to see Grandmama. To our surprise, Grandmama was about sixty pounds less than when we saw her the previous year. I remember looking at her. She was standing in the back room, where Granddaddy used to sleep. I was in the living room of the farmhouse. I looked down the hall and she was there cleaning. I just stared. She looked at me and we just stared at each other. It seem like five minutes, but actually was about twenty seconds. I looked at her face. It was covered with the pain of losing her baby boy. She was tired, and there was yet another death in the family. She looked like death was upon her. She made it through the viewing and funeral. Shortly after that, we headed back to Nashville to fly back to Orlando. I knew that it would not be long before the death angel would knock again.

Grandmama's health was slipping, and she started her trips back to the doctors. Good 'ol Mom was there to drive her to her appointments. Grandmama was hospitalized and had some observation done on her condition. Mom would be a flower by being there in this deep, depressing, lonely stage of Grandmama's life. The doctors had told Grandmama that there wasn't anything they could do for her. So, upon hearing that news, she asked the doctor if she could go home from the hospital. The doctors told Grandmama she could go if she had someone to help oversee her medication. Mom, being Georgia Taylor, volunteered. Mom would stay with her mom. She would cook, clean, give medicine, and do whatever needed to be done. This went on for several weeks. One day, while at her mom's bedside, Mom noticed that Grandmama's breathing was getting shorter. She lifted Grandmama up, and with her mom's fragile body in her hands she asked, "Are you leaving me?" Grandmama could not answer. "It's okay to go on home." And with that, Grandmama took her last breath in the arms of the one who loved her and cared for her. Mom was her flower in life and in death. Grandmama passed away five months after Tom. During the time of Tom's death and Grandmama's death, Mom had taken her life and put it on hold. She would stay with Grandmama, and then go home to look after Dad's needs. She would make that trip from her house to Grandmama's so many times, she could not even count them if she were asked.

Many say that Grandmama died from cancer. I know it was the pain of loneliness and heartache. The house of three was now gone.

Lloyd and I made the trip again to Tennessee. This time we drove. We had to work that day, then drive thirteen and a half hours to get home. We would take turns driving. Lloyd would drive and I would sleep, then we would switch places. I would drive until I could not hold my eyes open any longer. I would pull the car over, then call to Lloyd, "Your turn." We made it home, and paid our respects to our grandmother.

Little did we know that love so strong between sisters could cause the next event. While at the funeral services for Grandmama, Aunt Mer was getting sick. She had a bad cold. It was the dead of winter in Tennessee. Getting in and out of the cold for a person Aunt Mer's age took its toll. The emotional depression and the great loss of a sister placed Aunt Mer in the hospital the night of Grandmama's funeral. I was to be in Nashville the next morning for a meeting with the retail company I had joined. It was their annual meeting. It was my first meeting to attend. The other management team, in Florida, was coming to Nashville by chartered bus. I would meet with my manager at the hotel and attend the first meeting. Mom had been to the hospital to see Aunt Mer that night; she had been checked in and seemed to be okay. Mom and Mrs. Irene, her running buddy back and forth on the highway, were ready to take me to my meeting, in Nashville. Before we could go, we had to check in with Aunt Mer. So the three of us headed to the hospital the next morning. Aunt Mer was in good spirits and carried on with us. Before leaving, I leaned over to Aunt Mer and gave her a kiss on the lips—the first time in my life. She said, "I don't know if I will be here the next time you come home." I told her she would, and to stop talking like that. She gave a smile as we headed out the door. There was someone there who was staying with Aunt Mer, but to this day, I can't remember who; just more old people around taking care of their own.

I believed that she would rebound after some rest in the hospital and be okay. I also knew that she was probably right about her fate. Mom and Mrs. Irene made it to Nashville and returned home safely. I made it to my meeting, and went back to Orlando a few days later with the rest of the team, on the chartered bus. Upon my return home, I called Mom to see how my aunt was doing. My mom, being flowers for her family again, had Aunt Mer living with her. The good thing about my meeting was that I received a bonus check! Yeah, three thousand two hundred dollars. I was excited. This was the most money I had ever had in my personal possession. A few weeks later, I flew to North Carolina to see my girlfriend, Sara Wakeley. I had scoped out the jewelry store for the past few months, anticipating that I could buy my future bride an engagement ring, and with the bonus money, I did. I made the trip with one thing on my mind: to ask Sara's dad if I could marry her.

I flew to the Asheville, North Carolina, airport on a Friday night. Sara was there to pick me up. We drove in the dark to the little town of Cullowhee. We arrived around eleven P.M. Her mom and dad were there and greeted me as usual, then shortly went to bed. Sara and I stayed up a little while and watched TV. I told her that I was going to ask her dad the next day if I could marry her. I solicited her help on what would be the best approach. We talked about the different responses that he could give, then we retired to our separate rooms and slept for the night.

Saturday morning we had breakfast. The Wakeleys had some company, and when they woke up, we all talked for a while. Sara and I retired downstairs to watch TV. To my surprise, her dad came down a few minutes later to watch TV. I gave Sara the nod and she left the room. I mustered the nerve to ask if I could speak to him about marriage. I said, "Mr. Wakeley, part of the reason for me coming here this weekend was to ask you a question."

He shut off the television and all attention was given to me. His sharp blue eyes cut through me.

I said, "I wanted to know if I could ask for your daughter Sara's hand in marriage?"

The wait was not long. He quickly responded, "I think that would be a good idea."

In my surprise, he spoke, but I could not tell you all that he said. After we finished our talk, he returned upstairs and I hunted for Sara. I found her and we went to the WCU, Western Carolina University, campus. Sara drove her mother's red Caravan. We parked on the campus, overlooking the running track. I got down on one knee in the van and asked, "Will you marry me?" Sara said, "Yes." We kissed and talked about plans for a little while, then we said that the next song on the radio that we agreed on would be our song. "I'll Be Dreaming," by Vanessa Williams, became our song.

Sunday, Sara and I flew back to Orlando. While there, we did some planning and dreaming. She stayed for five days. During this time, the phone rang one evening. It was Mom. Aunt Mer had just passed away, one month after her sister Louise. I remember crying on the phone and Sara coming over to hold me while talking to Mom. Sara had become my flower.

In a matter of one and a half years, there were four deaths. My mom had given her all to be the flowers for her family, in life and in death.

Chapter Seven
You Reap What You Sow

AS WE were growing up, it was so easy to see the tangible things we did not have compared with other families. Dad's drinking in the seventies drove any extra income to almost nothing.

Mom and Dad split up for three years. The drinking that was going on during this time was bootlegged moonshine. There were no regulations or inspections of these stills. The health damage that was ingested was unreal by today's standards. The height of Dad's drinking caused my parents to live better apart from each other. Another act of violence by Dad had forced Mom to involve the police. After his arrest, he told Mom to get out. She did. Mom found a place and moved on. She tried to make it on a limited income, and she continued working odd jobs to keep money coming in.

The three older siblings had married and started their own families. The three younger Taylor children started to work too. We would rake leaves, mow yards, run errands, pick cotton, or do whatever it took to make a dollar. We still had to go to school and try to make it there also. The one thing that we did realize was what the old people drilled into us: to get our education. We would complain some, but when Mom heard us, she used to tell us that you reap what you sow. If you don't do anything, then you don't reap anything. Pretty basic knowledge to live by.

Lloyd finished high school in 1978, and started working at a local factory. Al and I were in high school until the eighties. We all had the great pleasure of working at the Piggly Wiggly while in high school. We did not work there at the same time; however, it helped us to earn money to do things. I worked there some of my junior and senior years in high school. Thanks to the Stanfill family, the owners of the store, for trusting in us. I was going to become a physical therapist, and also worked at the local hospital in the physical therapy department to help make money. High school was not much of a challenge. I did not apply myself. So I graduated and then went to college.

I was not a drinker or a person who went to parties. I just wanted to go to school and start working. I made it through my first few years with fun and okay grades. My second year I had lost focus. I remember that I had to have a full year of chemistry, calculus, and physics. I started going to the library, but could not get the hang of it, so I had to face the truth: my high school lack of involvement had finally caught up to me. I changed my major to broadcasting. Things seemed to be on the rise in this field. I floated through my sophomore year. I started to drink a little bit and hang out. This hanging out led me to working as a disc jockey at a local nightclub in the latter part of my college career. To make a long story short, instead of graduating in four years, it took me closer to six.

There were no old people around to guide me and hold me accountable. I struggled to find the *me* that wanted to be someone. I think it was a struggle of economics more than anything. When I was at school, I felt that I could compete. When I went home on school breaks, I felt that I was stuck. While in school, I was working and learning new things, but when I came home, it was the same old thing.

My brother Al went to UT-Martin for a while, then transferred to UT-Knoxville. He graduated on time with an electrical engineering degree. He had a job offer the day of graduation. Mom tells the story that she and Dad were at Al's apartment. He had to go to the store for something before graduation, so he left, and while he was out, an Appalachian power company called and wanted to speak to him. Mom talked to the gentleman who had interviewed Al. He was very complimentary of him. He also had called to offer him a position and to tell him his starting salary. I had been working for about a year now at my job in retail, and I heard the amount he was going to make; it was almost twice the amount of my salary. I was happy for him. Al had always been smart, and he applied that to school and it paid off. After working for a while as an engineer, he went back to night school and earned his MBA.

Lloyd had finally had enough of the small-town life in

Lexington. He called an aunt of ours in Orlando and he asked if he could come down to visit and search for a job. She and her husband agreed. Lloyd took a vacation from his factory job and headed down to search for a job. During this time, Lloyd dated a young lady who just graduated from TSU. She went to Atlanta to look for a job the same time as Lloyd's trip. They checked in with each other to see how the job search was going. They had made plans for Lloyd to stop by her home on his trip back from Florida. On the way back, she had a fatal accident. Lloyd was emotionally crushed. He drove back thirteen hours to deal with what had happened.

After paying his respects and trying to deal with the unthinkable, he accepted a dishwashing job in Orlando. He moved in with his aunt and uncle. Aunt Cora was a nurse and also had other degrees. She married Uncle Bob. He was a dentist. This was not Cora and Bob's first marriage. They were married before, with children, and a history before they met. They had a lot of success together. They loved to play bridge and entertain others with nice bridge parties. They lived the good life in front of Lloyd. They shared with him the things that came along with some worldly success. They also taught him that this success did not come freely. It took hard work. They encouraged Lloyd to go to college and make something of himself. It was probably the lowest point in his life, as he realized that it was going to take more than good looks to make it in this world. Lloyd enrolled at UCF and earned his degree in psychology. He had a few jobs as he worked his way through school. He graduated from washing dishes to waiting tables at one of the Disney hotels.

At this point, all the Taylor children are doing okay. Brenda is married, with five children, and her husband is a bi-vocational pastor of a church. Robert Junior is chief electrician for a company in his hometown. He is married with three children and is deacon at his church. Margaret is divorced, and has two children. She is the executive director for a domestic violence education center. Margaret's daughter was the first doctor—a dentist—in the family. She graduated from the University of Tennessee with a degree in Health Sciences. Go Vols! Lloyd is a personnel director for a hotel, and is married with twins. Al is an engineer for an Appalachian power company, and I'm the store director for the retail chain I started with in 1985. I'm married and have four children.

Dad's years of hard living—his sowing—had taken its toll on him. In the late seventies, he started to have small seizures. They continued for a while, but he bounced back a bit and continued to work. He would always be busy. I remember Dad getting laid off because work was slow at his factory. I thought that maybe it was a good thing. He had been working at the factory and fixing televisions for years. This unexpected break might do him some good. I remember Dad would work at his shop, then come across the street (home) at the end of the day. He would have dinner, then sit and watch the Atlanta Braves baseball team. This was his team. He would grab a cup of coffee and watch the entire game, nightly. This was the first time I remember Dad's being happy. His walk was faster and he was excited to get to his chair in the living room to catch the game.

After the layoff went on for months, Dad did not make many trips back across the street to his shop. He sat there and watched TV from the time he got up to the time he went to bed. Dad would walk to the kitchen and get a cup of coffee. This continued all day, well into the night. He would sit and watch TV and not say much to anyone. He would enjoy his shows. Sometimes I would hear him chuckle. I remember thinking that Dad was slowing down. Dad was getting depressed.

While at home during a summer break from college, I remember one night, while in bed, I was having a dream. I was dreaming that Dad was having a heart attack. In my dream, Dad could not speak, but Mom was calling for me to come help him. I could hear mom calling, "Coleman ... Coleman!" As I was waking up from my dream, I heard Mom calling my name. I ran down the hallway to Mom and Dad's room, which was Papa's old room. I was yelling, "Mama!" She told me to calm down. As I got to the room, Dad was having a grand mal seizure. His body was shaking and he was coming off the bed. I caught Dad and laid him on he floor. He was breathing, and Al called 911. The EMT came and picked Dad up. Al and I drove the car, and Mom assisted Dad in the ambulance. We arrived at the hospital in Lexington three minutes later. Dad started to come back around. He wanted to pee really bad. He woke up, and just as if he had never missed a beat, said, "I need to pee!" So he did, in the little urinal in the emergency room. After Dad's bathroom break, he was fine. Dad returned home that night and went for tests at the doctor's office later that week. The final result of Dad's tests was that he was toxic. He was not eating right or drinking any water. He was consuming a lot of coffee. He changed his diet some, with the help of Mom. Over the next few years, Dad continued to have mild seizures from time to time, with no real diagnosis.

At this point in life, Mom and Dad were there alone. All the children had left the house and started their own families. There would be visits from each of the siblings at various times throughout the year. Sometimes making a visit back home became a mini family reunion.

As the families would return home to see Mom and Dad, the evidence of Dad's health problems was growing more pronounced. He began to shuffle his feet, instead of making full steps. It was as if he was running, but not making a lot of gain. His posture began to slump over. His eyes were more defined and bulged out further than before the seizures. Dad's health declined to a point where he could no longer work. This decline happened within a few years. Seems like the reaping came unexpectedly.

Mom, during this time, was involved with trying to help each of her children's families. She would baby-sit, or make curtains; just about anything to show her support for her children and their mates. She was there with Dad; they had time to talk and reflect without any distractions. It appeared that they were back on track, but just getting older. They made it to all the children's weddings over the years, and were involved with the progress of their grandchildren. Dad started to attend church, at Pilgrims' Rest Baptist Church. Mom later left her church and started attending church with Dad. They were a sight to see: Mom with her walker, Dad hunched over with his Bible, walking to church on Sunday morning. The church was only fifty yards away.

Through all the ups and downs with Mom and Dad's life, it appeared that they were going to make it. Raising six children, losing a set of twin girls to premature birth, and a host of things, were Mom and Dad's challenges. Throughout the years of dealing with physical disability, alcohol abuse, economic hardship, relationship dysfunction, and health issues, these two were going to enjoy their time together as man and wife, finally.

Chapter Eight
We Make Appointments

WITH ALL the Taylor children married with children of their own, routine daily life became somewhat normal. We were dealing with the same problems as the rest of America. We had our responsibilities in our new roles as fathers, mothers, church members, civic leaders, and role models. We had our duties with our jobs and positions. Life was good. A phone call every now and then was how we communicated. On our birthdays, we would get calls from the other siblings. This has become a treat. At least six times a year we check in on each other. If I did not receive a call from one of my brothers or sisters, I knew they must have had a busy day. Growing up we did not have birthday parties with visitors. We would get to choose our dessert. We could have cake, cookies, or whatever, plus ice cream for that day. Mom would make it for us. We would celebrate with our family. Over the years, this has become very special to me. I prefer intimacy with family on that day.

Face-to-face conversations would take place when visiting Mom and Dad's place. This would happen during the holidays; for most of the family, it was Christmastime. For me, working retail, it was other holidays when I could make it home. Each of the brothers and sisters would visit home. We were always welcome to come home. With six different schedules and spouse schedules to consider, it was very rare when we were all together. When we were together, we always had a great time. There was no drinking of alcohol or using any illegal substance. We just enjoyed each other's company. We would reminisce about the good old days. We would catch up on current events about each other's children and family stuff.

Mom would have a Sock-it-to-Me cake, a chocolate cake, red velvet cake, apple pie, fried chicken, greens, cornbread, potato salad, baked beans, and sweet tea when we would arrive. The house would light up. All the cousins would start playing, and things were at a high. Each family would bring something. There would be enough food to feed a neighborhood. We would cook out on some holidays, like the Fourth of July. Barbecue chicken, hamburgers, ribs, potato salad, baked beans, and the best smoked pork BBQ in the world would be on the menu.

Part of our conversation would be in private, about Dad. We would comment on how quickly his health had deteriorated. We would look at the two parents and try to do some planning about how to best take care of them. When one of us was brave enough to ask about future plans for them, we were quickly put in our place. "I guess we're the children now, we can't take care of ourselves?" Mom would respond. Dad never acknowledged the conversation. We, as children, would not consider a hostile takeover on their lives. We loved them and wanted the best for them. We let them work though their wants and desires for themselves.

It was a quiet, peaceful setting when you went home. Mom and Dad were there together. It appeared that they were just meant to be together. They had been through it all and loved each other very much. One of the sad parts about their being together was there were no distractions from keeping them from facing the truth—the truth about their past, the truth about their present, and the truth about their future.

One of the truths that needed to be settled was regarding the pregnant lady, before their marriage. Mom tells of the conversation about that lady. She asked Dad again, "Is this your child?" After forty-plus years, the answer was, "It may be my child." Mom wanted to know why Dad never told his children that he loved them. Mom asked Dad if he loved his children. He said, "I think so." She was puzzled by the answer. "What do you mean, I think so?" Dad began to tell of his childhood, how it was not proper for a man to show any affection to his children. Papa did not show any love toward Dad or his brother and sister. Papa had given his children to his sister to raise. He told Mom he did not know what love was. He was not taught to love. He shared a fond memory that Papa had come to Lexington via train. He had brought a red wagon with him. Papa pulled Dad and his brother home from the train station. This was one of his memories of love. This type of behavior for Papa was common for his generation. This was passed on to Dad. I never heard Dad say I love you. I knew that he did. I did not waste time trying to get Dad to say those three words. Sometimes we can hear with our eyes, the old people used to say. They had time to settle their lives, and time to settle the truth. It was a joy to come home.

We make appointments and God makes disappointments was a saying I saw come to life. In my career, I was asked to go to Anchorage, Alaska, to work for the retail company. At this point, I had been working for the company for seven years. I remember getting a call one day on my voicemail. The message was asking me to return a call about a possible position in Alaska. They asked me to please call back so that we could talk about this. I returned the call as a professional courtesy. I told personnel that they had the wrong guy. Headquarters for the retail company was located in Arkansas, so when I received the call, I thought it was a cattle call for souls to go to the last frontier. I told them that at this point, I didn't even own a coat. I lived in Orlando, Florida; I had no interest in going to Alaska. After a friendly conversation, we ended our phone call. The next day I received another call asking me to go to Alaska. One of the old people's sayings was that opportunities don't always knock twice. So I returned the call with an inquisitive ear. I asked detailed questions about the store, and was told it was a rough situation that needed some energy and training. At this point, I was completing two years in a position that required a lot of travel. I was a field trainer with the company and traveled around the United States facilitating classes. It was the perfect job for me. I enjoyed it and got good responses from the classes. Sara and I were parents now, with one child, Lauren, and at this point, it was better for me to be home to help raise our child. I was about a month from returning to the stores to work in operations. I had just had the best two years in my career. The recruiter was asking for a two-year commitment. I asked what position, and he told me that I would be a co-manager for a store in Anchorage. I told him that in a month I was returning to the stores in Orlando as a co-manager. The way I saw it, I was not gaining anything in this deal. I told him that I would talk it over with my wife and entertain the thought.

I called Sara at her job. I told her that I needed to talk to her and asked if we could do lunch. It was always a treat to see Sara during the day. I picked her up and we went to an Italian restaurant for lunch. I remember the first twenty minutes of the conversation, asking each other little tidbits of information about Anchorage. We found out that we had very little information. The next twenty minutes of the conversation were, what if we go to Alaska? Two years would fly by if we were having fun. If it did not turn out to be fun, we could just stick it out and return back home after our tour of duty. Alaska was far enough away to just be crazy enough to do it. The last twenty minutes were, when do we go to Alaska?

We agreed to go and work for two years at store 2070. Sara, Lauren, and I were on our way to a new life. My appointment was to work in Orlando the next month. God's disappointment was to go to Alaska. We went for six and a half years. At this point, in the nineties, things seemed all right. Dad's health had been a growing issue, and how to cope with the issues of aging parents was the underlying subject for all the children. At this point, Dad's health had been failing for more than twenty years. It started with the small seizures, then larger ones. Along the way, doctors had told him that he had had some small strokes. Having small strokes was normal with his condition. These small seizures happened from time to time, and the family grew to accept them. Dad was on medication that helped to control his episodes most of the time, until December 8,1998, when he had a major stroke. When I first heard of Dad's stroke, I thought he would bounce back as he had done so many times in life. This time he did not. Mom made the decision to take care of her husband, no matter what. She had done it before, with her mom, brother, and others. She knew that it was a bad stroke.

Old people don't get old by being fools. This wisdom is very deep. I found out my view on life has been enhanced by this wisdom. It's the guide of wisdom passed on by the old people. Mrs. Maggie Jones would share a saying, a nugget of wisdom, with my mother and me when she used to visit our home from time to time. One of her sayings was, "We make appointments; God sometimes makes disappointments." This saying became very evident during my father's health struggles. My Dad's birthday was December 8, and I was going to call him on December 7 to wish him a happy birthday. I was living in Alaska and had worked till five P.M. Alaska time. This would have been eight P.M. in Tennessee. I wanted to call him after dinner, before it got too late in Tennessee. The next day I was to work a full schedule: seven A.M. to ten P.M. I knew that most days when I closed, I would become very busy, and I might not get the chance to call Dad on his birthday. We ate dinner and did the usual stuff in the Taylor household. I looked up and it was already eight o'clock.

"I'll call Dad tomorrow, Sara, it's too late in Tennessee now for me to call." I later went to bed. Like so many years before, the late night news would carry the film clip about the date that will live in infamy. That would always remind me that Dad's birthday was the following day. I cut off the television and slept. On his birthday, in 1998, he awoke and had a massive stroke. Mom recalls that Dad was able to speak when it first happened. She asked him, "You're having a stroke, do you know what is going on?" Dad responded, "Yes." Dad was taken to Memphis, to the Veterans Hospital. The first appointment for me was to call Dad the day before his birthday and wish him a happy birthday. The disappointment was ahead. December 8, 1998, I went to work as normal. I received a call from Mom at work. This is highly unusual. I answer the phone at the service desk. Mom told me that Dad had had a bad stroke. God's disappointment. I have thought so many times that, after Mom's phone call, I wish I would have called Dad on the seventh. She told me not to come to Tennessee. It was a long flight and there was nothing that I could do to help at this point. This is the only time that I ever felt distance between the rest of my family and me in the lower forty-eight. My family and I were so used to flying in and out of Alaska, because flying was the main mode of travel. At this point, I was a general manager for the retail company, which I had been with since 1985. It was the holiday season, and many things hinged on the performance of my store in December. I did not go to Tennessee that month. Dad survived the initial phase of the stroke. He had total paralysis and could not speak. He had a feeding tube in his nose. He had a tracheal tube in his throat. He had a catheter. I was to attend a yearly meeting in Kansas City, Missouri, in January of 1999. Before I went to this meeting, Dad was released to go home. He was dependent on care from others, mainly my mom. Before attending this meeting, I received a call from the regional office telling me to change my tickets after the meeting in Kansas City to take three days and go visit my mom and dad. I would only be a few hundred miles away versus a few thousand. I made the arrangements and had my travel all lined up. During the meeting in Kansas, I had the surprise of my career. My store was selected regional store of the year. I was given an award and a ring.

The timing was right. I walked into the house with Mom. She was glad to see me and I was glad to see her. I could tell that stress had taken its punches at Mom. She had aged years. I had seen her only a few months ago, during summer vacation. I walked into the house. It was quiet, and just Mom was there with Dad in the back bedroom. The Veterans Administration had set up a hospital bed and the necessary supplies. The walk down the hallway was the longest, saddest, and loneliest walk of my life. Dad lay there, the oxygen machine humming. I looked at my dad. His eyes wandered and I was able to make contact with them. Dad's eyes were unique because they were blue. The total iris wasn't just the outer edge of his iris. I said, "Hey, Dad, it's me, Coleman." As our eyes met, he had tears streaming down his face. Mom was behind me, being strong. She reached over and pulled out a tissue and wiped Dad's tears. I cried too. "Don't worry, Dad, we're going to get through this," I said. What was Dad thinking? Could he really hear me? Was it just a coincidence with the tears? How long would it be before Dad passed away? The thoughts that went through my mind were numerous. I was wearing my new ring from the meeting. This brought up a current event to share with Dad. I thought that maybe Dad would be proud of me if I showed him my award and ring. I went down the hall and got my suitcase. I pulled out the award and held my ring. "Daddy, I won regional store of the year!" I said, with tears in my eyes, my throat choking up. I knew he could hear me, and I knew that he was proud of me.

My mom made the decision that she would take care of Dad. When this first started, the VA visited twice daily. They would send a nurse and nurse's aide. They would check vital signs and bathe Dad. This had multiple purposes. First, it was care for my dad. Second, it was company for my mom. Mom and Dad were empty nesters. I learned very quickly why the stress had kicked Mom in the teeth after my first night there. Dad had a tracheal tube in his throat. This is a plastic tube that is inserted through the skin, through the trachea, to allow the person to breathe. This has multiple uses: one was to help keep Daddy from choking on his own phlegm. There is a machine that is used to suction out the trachea tube. Mom gave me a quick lesson the first afternoon that I visited. This job is not for the weak at heart. The suction sound is loud and uncommon. It sounds like something out of a medical movie with bad sound effects. The phlegm comes out of the tracheal tube to a collection container. I watched Mom suction Dad out several times during the afternoon. I wanted to help and give Mom a break while I was there for three days. I attempted to pitch in and do what I could with Dad.

Mom's nightly routine would be to make sure Dad was clean. She would check for soiled sheets and bedcovers. She would check Dad's bed pad. She would make sure Dad was in a comfortable position. She would check for any bed sores. Mom would talk to Dad in the most loving ways. She would love him and take care of every little detail for him. She would pray with Dad nightly and kiss him and tell him good night. Just as soon as Mom got into bed, Dad would cough. This would result in the tracheal tube making a loud gurgling sound, loud enough to wake you from your sleep. Dad would do this from time to time. It might be twice an hour, or four or five times per hour. Mom would get up. I wanted to help, so I started getting up during the night. I was tired from meetings, traveling, and emotions. I got up once: Mom was already up during the night. I got up again during the night. I successfully suctioned Dad out, and Mom got to sleep. The next morning, being proud of my accomplishments, I said, "I got up and took care of Daddy last night. He seemed to sleep better after I suctioned him out the last time."

Mom replied, "I heard you when you got up last night, but I don't think you budged at all the last two times I got up this morning."

I remarked to Mom that I did not hear a thing, or I would have gotten up. She made me feel good about what I did anyway. We had breakfast and waited for the nurse and aide to come.

I remember sitting there at the kitchen table, thinking, how long can anyone do this? I was tired from the two times I got up. Mom was beginning her second month taking care of Dad. How long could she last?

Chapter Nine
God Makes Disappointments

THE VETERANS Administration was a wonderful help. They gave Dad medical attention while he was in the hospital, and the needed items to take care of him when he returned home. There were the daily supplies for survival: a hospital bed, diapers, bed pads, suction machine, and an array of tubes and supplies to keep him alive. The No Revitalize clause, for Mom, was not an option. She wanted to do everything in her power for her husband. Knowing Mom, if something had happened to him while under her care, at home, she would not have forgiven herself. Very often Mom would make calls to the VA to get the needed items. She was the medic in the home, ready for action at anytime.

I witnessed this regimented soldier not leave her post. While visiting with Mom and Dad, while on vacation, she would not go anywhere. Every now and then she might go to church, if one of the trusted children were at home. I asked Mom who did the grocery shopping for her. Her answer, "me." I asked when and how she went shopping. She shared with me that when the nurse would come in daily, she would go to the store for twenty minutes. She would have her money and shopping list and head to the store. Good thing it was a small town. I knew there was no way that she would last long; maybe a month or two, before she calls for the help of a nursing home. Again, this was a last-ditch effort, if at all, for her. The lady would use every muscle to turn Dad and clean him. She would change his urine bag. She would change his bed pads when soiled. She would change his sheets when they were dirty. She would roll Dad to make sure he was comfortable for the night. When I was there, I would help her, but when she was alone, it was all Georgia Taylor. Till death do us part, for better or worse; these are not just words spoken at the height of passion; these are words confirmed with a devoted action of love. No matter what, Mom was going to take care of her man, her groom.

As time went on, things seemed to be settling in for Mom. I thought of a project that might keep her mind off the daily house sitting. Sara and I had purchased Aunt Mer's place a year before Dad's stroke. Her place had three and a half acres. Her house was still on the property. James had moved in with Aunt Mer after the ax incident with Granddaddy George. After Aunt Mer passed away, James continued to live there. The property was willed to her niece. She was my mom's sister. The reason for this was a family skeleton. Aunt Mer never had children. Aunt Mer loved her husband. While her niece was living with them while going to school, the unthinkable happened. Her niece got pregnant. The father of the baby was Aunt Mer's husband. She was a young teenage girl, and Aunt Mer felt guilty for that event happening. So in her will, she left the place to her. This niece passed away in the early nineties. I had told Mom to inquire about the property with my cousins. I wanted to buy the property if no one was interested in it. Sara and I were able to buy the home.

Aunt Mer's house was falling down by this time, in 1999. I wanted to place a trailer on the property so that the renter would take care of the land and not let it become an overgrown property. Overgrown property is a common sight in rural Tennessee. This happens when no one has cut the grass and the house falls in. It looks like history stopped and time kept going. So I inquired about a trailer at the local bank. Sara and I purchased it. I wanted Mom to take over and get things going for me; get the old house torn down, get the new trailer put up on the property, get a renter in the house. I think I hit gold with this. I never saw anyone in my career handle money and business so tightly. I believe she could have done business with Donald Trump and won. She was successful at getting all the needed things lined up. She was as happy as I was seeing the events lined up each day. I noticed that while talking with her on a weekly basis; she had high spirits. This was almost like a hobby for her now. She would give me the blow by blow on all the details. She would call me if the rent was a day late. She would recount the conversation that took place about that piece of business. The renter always came through. This kept up for about a year. As Dad's condition did not change for better or worse, her energy was getting less.

When my family and I would visit on vacation, I could see that Mom was getting tired. She started going to the doctor for everything. She did catch the early onset of skin cancer, and had it removed. She had an obsession with her health. If it wasn't her heart, it was her stomach. Each phone call became routine: "Hello, Mom, how's Dad ?" Then she would tell me what was going on with her health. I asked several times to let the other children and me help, but she would not budge. She stated that this was what she was going to do. If she could not handle it, she would let us know. I asked on several occasions what I could do to help, and each time the same answer was the same: "Nothing; just keep me in your prayers."

My sisters and brothers would talk about how to help, but there was no winning with Mom. If she was going to do something, no one could stop her. Four years and eleven months had passed, and Mom's health was still an issue. She was finally scheduled for a cardiogram, to see if there was something really going on with her heart. The local doctors had ruled out every possible thing. When one doctor did not give her the answer she wanted, she would switch doctors. Her reasoning was that the doctors did not know what they were talking about. So, after getting to the final point of truth with her health, she was going to see if she was really sick.

I remember calling all my brothers and sisters the week before her cardiogram. We needed to make a decision. We needed to be prepared for what might come with these test results. All were in agreement that we would react when the test results came back. The general consensus was that if Mom was sick and had to have surgery, we would have to take Dad to a nursing home or have a home nurse. The home-nurse option would not set well with Mom, but we would have to do what we would have to do. Mom's logic, in all of her thoughts, was not to inconvenience any of her children. We all had families that needed us, and not to compromise our families. The children were in agreement. Mom would have to take a different role. I was ready for her to move in with me. Sara was ready to do the right thing. We were ready for whatever it took. Robert and Brenda were ready for whatever it took. Lloyd, Margaret, and Al were ready to do their part.

The procedure was to take place on Monday. Much to our surprise, Mom had called the hospital on Sunday night. She complained about her heart and how it was hurting her. The hospital had
advised her to come to the Emergency Room. She did. They kept
her. Margaret had stayed with Mom to keep an eye on her to get her
to her appointment on Monday. It was a good thing that Margaret
was there to help with Mom's alleged emergency. The real truth
about the situation was that Mom felt that if the she was in the hospital, she would not have to go to her cardiogram the next day.
Worn out and tired, but still slick as a fox; Mom wanted attention
and she was going to get it on Monday morning. She has been trying to be ill for a long time. Every doctor had started to close the
doors to her, and she was not getting the answers she wanted. In this
case, maybe the truth was the scariest factor that could happen to
mom. If she really was sick, she would have to face the truth and
let others help her with Dad. For the first time, she would have to
admit failure, in trying to take care of Dad. So, not taking the test
would prove she was still viable to do her duty as a love warrior for
her husband. Well, to Mom's surprise, the doctor asked the ambulance to take Mom to the hospital in Jackson to do the cardiogram
the next morning. Brenda had come to take Mom to the doctor, and
Margaret stayed with Dad at home. Mom had her cardiogram. She
was healthy.

Mom was released Monday afternoon. Brenda accompanied
her home and stayed with her. Mom had some pain from the inci-
sion in her leg. I called to check on her, and she seemed to be all
right. Tuesday rolled around, and I had to close; I would be at work
all day and night. I did not make contact with her that day.
Wednesday came, and I visited with Mom on the phone. She
seemed to be okay. There was almost a routine tone back in her
voice. "How's Dad?" She responded, "He looks sad. I think he
missed me when I was in the hospital. Margaret was here with me,
and he slept through the night." Margaret was staying over
Wednesday night to help Mom with her transition.

For me, that day was a full one. On November 12, 2003, I woke
up around eight A.M. It was my day off. I took my two oldest children to school, then came home and had breakfast with Sara. The

two smaller children were at home playing and having fun. They watched their favorite cartoons, and at eleven we started our daily routine, getting ready for preschool. Our third child started school at twelve-thirty. Sara and I had peanut butter and jelly sandwiches with apple juice. After lunch, Sara started with the preschooler's hair and clothes. Sara loaded the two young children in the van and went off to school. It was a beautiful day, with blue skies and a perfect temperature. I went on the back patio, by the pool, and lay in the sun for about forty-five minutes. In the meantime, our youngest was asleep, so Sara joined me for some sun. Wednesday is early-release day, so we ended our sunning. We loaded up our youngest and headed back to pick up the two oldest. We leave at one-thirty each Wednesday. If you have children, you understand the logistics it takes to get to the front of the line to pick up your children. We did this each Wednesday. After picking them up, we have just a short time to pick up our preschooler. We then would head back home to get snack and check on any homework. Then it's back out again to pick up the only chick out of the nest. We get everyone home. Our rule is homework first. So the children start on their homework, while the two youngest play. Wednesday is parenting night for me and the two youngest. Sara has a sign-language class at the church, and the two oldest children have different classes at the church.

Tonight I wanted to be on the ball. I played with the children and watched a short video with them. I wanted to get the holiday letter printed and ready to go in the mail the Wednesday before Thanksgiving, so I was hustling to get this done. I went to the computer and printed out the letter. We had twenty-two people on our list. I printed twenty-two, two-page letters on Christmas holiday paper. I placed them in a nice neat pile and got the matching envelopes to the paper. I folded the letters and placed our family Christmas portrait inside. I bathed the children for the night and got them ready for bed, but as on every other Wednesday, they wanted to wait up for their mother to come home, so we watched another video, and then placed stamps and preprinted return-address stickers on all the Christmas letters. I put them on the fireplace mantle. I was really proud of myself that night.

Sara and the rest of the gang came home, and I let the children join in for a while. Wednesday is a long day for them. The two who were with me, I let them have at their mom. Hugs and kisses are always one of their delights when their mom comes home.

As the young ones headed up the stairs to bed, Sara and I had our nightly cup of coffee. We sat in the family room on the couch. I pointed up to the mantle. She asked, "What is that?" I told her about my night. Like a little boy wanting the approval of his mom, I sat back and watched her face, with signs of happiness. Sara gave the appropriate praise for her multitasking husband's work. We finished our coffee and headed upstairs. We read a book and said prayers with the children. After tucking them in, we went back downstairs to get ready for bed. We did our nightly ritual, and off to bed we went.

The night was an interesting night. I had very vivid dreams, and so did Sara. The next morning I woke up before Sara and did my morning routine. I showered and dressed in the master bathroom, then I went to the kitchen and read a chapter in my bible, then prayed. I remember Sara coming into the kitchen and giving me a hug. I asked her how she slept. She said okay. I told her that I had a great night of sleep. I had a dream that this man who had never been camping came by the house. I was working in the garage, and he walked up to me and we started talking. He told me that he was going camping. I have enjoyed camping since I was a little boy, and grew to love it more while in Alaska. So when I heard this I said, "You've never been camping? Boy, you'll have a great time!" I was looking at my camping gear and getting things to give to this man so that he could take it on his trip. I explained that the feeling of the fresh air, and the food, while camping, would do wonders for him. I asked him if I could go with him? He said no. His answer did not hurt me, but I said, "Maybe I can come later?" He nodded his head. "When we get there, we can do some fishing!" I made the casting motion with my hand, and the man headed back down the sidewalk. As I was telling Sara about this, I was excited, and wanted to go camping and fishing.

Sara said, "I had a bad dream."

"What did you dream about?"

She said, "Don't get mad, but I had a dream that I had an affair."

I said, "Let's hope that doesn't come true."

Sara and I talked a little while, and then I headed off to work. It was a short drive to work, only about ten minutes. I arrived at work and started my daily routine. I walked the sale floor and stock rooms. The store looked good, as it was two weeks before Thanksgiving. I was near the front of the store when I heard my walkie-talkie: "Coleman, it's your wife on line one." When I picked up the phone, Sara asked if I was sitting down. The thoughts of her dream came to mind. Is she going to drop a bomb on me? I was wondering why she'd let me get to work before calling me about something like this. I answered, "No, I'm standing in the jewelry department, what's up?"

Sara said, "Your sister just called, and your dad passed away this morning."

I don't know if it was the relief of Sara not giving me news about an affair, or if I really did not understand what she just told me. I responded, "Thank you, Sara, thank you for calling." And I hung up the phone.

I called the morning meeting and carried on as usual. The meeting is a daily recap for the associates about sales and the direction for the day. It normally runs about fifteen minutes. I had not told anyone at this point. After the meeting, I went outside and called Mom. My sister Margaret answered. She gave me the brief details: when the nurse came in this morning, Dad was already gone. I asked how Mom was taking it, and she said okay. I asked to speak to her. Mom said, "I knew he looked like he missed me while I was in the hospital this week. I had no idea that he was leaving me." I explained that God knew. If Dad would have died under someone else's care, she would not have forgiven them nor herself. Even if Dad would have died while she was taking care of him, she would not have forgiven herself. God took Dad home in the middle of the night. It wasn't anything Mom did or did not do. It was Dad's time to go. Then the walls of emotion came crashing down on me. My sisters, brothers, and I had been making appointments for how to help take care of Dad, but God's disappointment was that we did not have to make any decisions at all; He did.

I went back into the store. I called the management team together and told them what had happened. I made arrangements and left the store. After arriving home, I remembered my dream. The man in my dream did not leave with any of my camping gear that I was giving him to use on his trip. My wife's feeling of an affair was because another man was in the house that night. That other man was my Dad. He had come to pay a visit before he went home.

Chapter Ten
Old People Do Get Old

AS LIFE would have it, I was in Orlando when my Dad died. Lloyd, his family, and my family made arrangements and headed back to Tennessee; this time in separate cars, with many new additions to our families. I had my four daughters and wife, and Lloyd had his twin daughters and wife. Several thoughts accompanied my ride that day. How would my children react to a funeral? How would this impact me? How would this impact my Mom? How would I react to Dad's empty hospital bed? These thoughts were with me for several miles on our trip home. This is an all-day trip, with not much to view along the way. We had some great news while driving, though. I received a call from my brother Al. He and his wife had a baby boy. Al remained in Ohio until his mother-in-law arrived. She would help with the transition from the hospital to home with her daughter. Al would make the trip the next day, in time for the funeral.

As we drove, Sara and I thought about the wide range of emotions Al would deal with in just a few days: hearing the news that his dad had died; his wife going into labor and delivering a new baby; leaving his wife and five children to make an eight-hour drive by himself to the funeral services.

The ten of us made this trip without a hitch. We made the caravan to Lexington, to the same plot of land where Mom had lived for more than fifty years. The house was different from the one I grew up in during the sixties and seventies. Mom and Dad had gone to see about a loan in 1992 to repair their home. The old house was in such bad shape that the bank suggested they build a new house. They did. They moved into their new house in 1993. This was an answer to prayer for me. I had asked God to provide Mom and Dad with a new house many years before. One of the old people's sayings was, *God doesn't answer your prayer when you want, but He is always on time.*

Upon our arrival, I could only think of the hospital bed where Dad had lain for almost five years. To my surprise, when I walked down the hallway and looked into the room, the hospital bed was gone and the room was redecorated. I asked Mom what happened to the room. My brother Robert and sister Brenda had been at work. The stained walls, where Mom's handprints had been from steadying herself while walking, were painted. The carpet was replaced. The bed that Mom and Dad had used for many years was back in the place where the hospital bed used to be. The room was clean and different from when I last saw it, in the summer.

The ten of us checked in with Mom. We talked with her and had a briefing on the events of the day. Mom gave us the details for the day and the agenda for the next day. She asked if one of us would go to the funeral home in the morning to greet friends at the viewing. I agreed to be there early. Mom was worn out. The arrangements were already made for Dad's viewing and funeral. The sisters and brother who lived in Tennessee had assisted Mom, and the arrangements were made. Mom seemed to be in good spirits, considering the events of that week.

There was a huge amount of food in the kitchen. This was a common event for the local people, to assist the grieving family. There were cakes, hams, chicken, and all sorts of food to munch. We sat down, had a bite to eat, and then headed off to our hotels. As we were packing up to go to our car, I noticed that Mom was by herself. I asked my oldest child, Lauren, if she would stay with her grandmama. She said yes. She was ten years old at the time. I gave her instructions how to call me on the cell phone, and to help Grandmama if she needed anything. We headed out to the Pin Oak Lodge and settled in for the night.

The next day we were up early and had our clothes picked out for the day. We had Lauren's outfit with us and had her change clothes at Mom's. Sara, Mom, and I went to the funeral home. As we walked in, there was Dad's coffin. It had an American flag draped over it. There were a few plants around the coffin. I stared at Dad, and he looked good. He had on a dark blue suit with a matching necktie. I placed my hand on his hand and had my cry. I sat down in the front row of pews at the funeral home. Mom and Sara consoled me, and when I felt better, they left me to attend to the others at the house. I was left there alone with Dad. The funeral attendant was in his office working. He would look in on me from time to time. I stared at Dad and talked to him softly. I discovered that the cramped look from Dad's stroke was gone; he looked good. He was thinner than I remembered him when he was able to walk, but his facial expression was good. I remember thinking, *the pain is gone. Dad is at rest.* He had suffered for a long time and now he is free from that suffering. I talked to him and let him know that I just wanted him to hug me, I just wanted him to be proud of me, and even though he did not verbally say it, I knew it.

As I sat there, friends of Dad's came by to visit. Some were old people that I remembered growing up, and others I did not know. They told me stories of Dad. They laughed and explained how Dad wanted to be a pool shark. They shared how he would show up at the pool hall first on Saturday mornings to shoot pool. They told me stories of his nickname, Gennis; this is what Dad used to call money. I never knew that. As I sat there, I was amazed that these old people knew what to say. The men who came by shared the goodness of Dad, and they laughed true laughs. I saw smiles on their faces as they would share some of their old times with me. It made me want to go back and be there at that time, if I could. The stories of Dad and these men showed me the impact on their lives in a positive way. These men knew how I was feeling, and their stories made me proud of my Dad that day. What I thought was going to be a day of gloom turned out to be a day of celebration of my dad. I sat there for five hours until my brother Lloyd came to relieve me. The official wake was to begin at six P.M.

During the wake, a time for friends to come by and pay their respect to the family, there were many things I wanted to say, but to whom? Many of Mom and Dad's friends came to pay their respects to Dad. This was a quiet time, and many of my brothers' and sisters' friends came by also. During the wake, there were many emotions attached to it; the realization that Dad's life did touch others, and that there was more to my dad than I knew. Through his family, he reached out and touched many people. The other emotion was seeing family and friends that I had not seen in years. I was glad to see them, and just their being there made a huge difference in dealing with my father's death.

The wake lasted for about two hours, and during this time, I was moved deeply to tears. I hadn't cried much during my adult years, except during the birth of my children. The crying I experienced was more of a deep mourning. I noticed that others in my family did not feel so moved. I know they were feeling the same loss I did, and I wondered what was going on with them. I felt that I needed to deal with this loss now, or it would come out in a different way than I needed. I was concerned that I would resort to heavy drinking, or that life would just seem useless. My cry was needed to let my soul deal with the truth that there was nothing I could do to change the past.

Next the funeral was held at my parents' church, Pilgrim Rest Baptist Church. Some of the old people who were around when I grew up were still there, in the same pews. The church had a great service, and the message was, *everything that looks bad, ain't bad*. It was a way to look at death as a part of life, the end of life on earth. For a believer in Jesus Christ, it is not a bad day, but a glorious day. This day would be the beginning of eternity. Pastor White told a story about my Dad. He spoke of Dad's spiritual salvation and his return to the church after that. He shared that Dad did not sit in the back of the church; he came up to the Amen corner, a place where the elderly men would sit and pray during the church service. Dad knew that he was a new person, and he acted like it. He spoke of the day that Dad asked if he could pray in the church service. The pastor said he agreed to let Dad pray. Pastor White encouraged others who may have strayed from the church to come back to the church. During the service, my children were broken. Their tears fell like flowing water. Their little hearts were broken. Looking at them, I had to be strong. I placed my arm around them and sang softly under my breath. The song "I'll Fly Away" played through the service and I would find comfort by singing it. As this part of the service ended, we proceeded out to our cars. We drove in single-car formation to the cemetery.

The service ended at the Lexington cemetery, where my Dad had a military guard standing at his grave site. There was a soldier standing like a statue in front of my father's coffin, which had an

American flag draped over it. At the appointed time, the soldier and my nephew Chad, an active marine, folded the flag. The soldier brought the flag over in traditional style and presented it to Mom. The honorable words spoken to Mom on behalf of the United States government were clear and respectful. Mom received the flag, with me sitting next to her.

When the pastor finished the service, we all left the grave site as the funeral director lowered Dad's coffin into the ground. Many were huddled together as they made their way back to their cars. As I walked with my wife and children, I noticed a great friend of mine, Walter Pope, with his wife and two of his younger children. Walter and I started school the same year, 1969. We completed grade school, high school, and college at the same schools. Walter is a white American, and I am a black American. We always had respect for each other. To see this man and his family at the grave site showed me again the power of how my parents raised me. In a small southern town, it doesn't take long to see who your friends really are. Walter has always been a friend. Through the many years of racial unrest, tension in our country, and peer pressure, Walter and I remained friends.

I noticed the soldier who stood by Dad's grave. I wanted to thank him for his service and commend him on the way he handled the funeral duty. As I looked at him, I recognized him. He was someone I had gone to school with many years ago, Benny. His impact and the professionalism he presented sealed the importance of life. At this point, Dad's life was honored and the time he served in World War II was not forgotten. My fears of Dad's being forgotten were overwhelmingly overcome. The old people and the newly old people made a difference at the lowest point in my life.

We went back to the church. After a funeral, there is a reception for the family. The reception is to feed those who have traveled and worked the funeral service. It is one of the sweetest times during a funeral service. It is a way to see friends and loved ones who have supported you over the years. There was so much food, and the faithful old people at the church waited on our every need. There were cousins I had not seen in twenty years. Some of them had children and grandchildren. It was a time to just relax from the formal setting of the services.

While sitting down and visiting with friends and family, I had the surprise of my life. An older lady came over and shook my hand and said, "Hi, my name is Linda; I'm your half sister." I responded, "Hello, my name is Coleman." She already knew my name and my brothers' and sisters' names. She spoke about Dad as her dad. I did not let this bother me. As she spoke, I was looking at her features. She had eyebrows like my Dad. Her nose looked like my brother Al's and my sister Margaret's. Her skin color was a little darker than mine. Not knowing her mother, the skin color would be right. During my brief conversation with her, I accepted her as my sister. At this point, there was nothing I could do to see if she was right. It did not matter. I started to wonder about her. If this really was Dad's daughter, what deep, severe, emotional pain she had gone through for many years. Dad was gone, and if this was his child, how would he want me to treat her? I did what Dad would have me do: I treated her like a sister. We spoke a few more minutes and then went our separate ways. I mingled with a few more friends. My wife and children headed back to Mom's house, and I drove Mom home. It was a good time—a celebration of my Dad's life.

The immediate family all gathered back at Mom's. We shared thoughts before many headed back to their homes. Lloyd's family and mine stayed for a while, chatting. Sara and I had checked out of our hotel that morning and planned to stay with Mom before leaving early the next day. As we sat there, my thoughts were very heavy about Mom. I looked at her. The bags under her eyes were dark and deep. She kept placing her right hand to her forehead. Her fingers would rub her wrinkles back and forth. She was almost defeated. I knew she needed time to grieve. Lloyd and his family were staying at a hotel for one more night, and then would stay one more day with Mom. How long would it take Mom to bounce back? Now that she had completed this mission in life, would she come visit me in Florida? I had already planned my vacation for the first week of January. This is a time I choose each year to share with my children, before they go back to school. I made a mental note that I could use some of that time to fly back and see Mom. My thoughts were that the holidays would be over and the quietness would be setting in after the New Year. I had figured that the timing would be perfect. As we all sat there recalling the good days of old, I was making plans to assist Mom on a goodwill visit.

We slowly started packing our stuff that night; Lloyd and his family had left for their hotel. Sara slept in Dad's old bedroom with our youngest daughter; I slept on the couch. We had to get up early and head back to Florida in the morning. I had to get ready for the holiday season. Thanksgiving was only about two weeks away, and the Christmas shopping season would begin the day after that. The rest of the family had school and other commitments. Sara is a stay-at-home mom. She is co-leader of a Brownie troop, a homeroom mom for preschool, a preschool worker at church, involved in sign-language class, a taxi cab for rehearsals for the Christmas play, and a homemaker. Her plate was full. We woke up early, loaded up the family, said our goodbyes, and left for Orlando.

We made it home safely, and got back into our routine. When I started my routine, it was an emotional roller coaster. It seemed that things were back to normal, except for the occasional sneak attack of emotions. When I was driving in my car, a song would come on the radio and remind me of my father. Looking at my children would bring up memories of my father. I would think to myself, *I wonder what Dad would think when he looked at us playing. Was he happy?* This would bring up emotions that were totally unexpected.

We had planned for the holidays. We made it through Thanksgiving and Christmas. I would make a couple of phone calls to Mom each week. Mom did not fare well. Her behavior, shared by brothers and sisters around her children during the holidays, was strange. She wanted to stay at home. She would fulfill her invitation to visit and would complain that she did not feel well. She would make comments that were not proper for her. She felt paranoid about her son and daughters. My sisters and brother thought it was depression and that she was still dealing with the recent loss of Dad.

The invitation for Mom to spend the Thanksgiving holiday at Brenda's was twofold: one reason was just to have her there, and the other was to get Mom around others and lift her spirits. During her visit, Mom showed some behavior that was just plain weird. She stated that she was tired. Brenda told Mom to go get changed and go to bed. Mom had difficulty getting her clothes off. Brenda went to help her and Mom got hysterical. She was complaining that she could not get her slip off. When Brenda lifted the slip over her head, Mom thought Brenda was trying to strangle her.

I just wanted to keep in touch with her to see how things were going. She seemed to be okay, but was feeling the loss of her husband. I knew this was natural, especially for someone who had been in a relationship for over fifty years; there would obviously be a void.

As the new year rolled around, I made a planned trip back to Tennessee. Sara and I had planned for this for a few weeks. Sara had given me her total support to deal with Mom. I flew to Tennessee without Sara or the children. My sister Margaret and her friend Norman picked me up at the Nashville airport. It was a late flight. I arrived at ten-forty P.M. We drove into Lexington and talked about many different things. Mom, of course, was one of the subjects that came up. Margaret had mentioned that Mom had changed since Dad died. Margaret told me about how Mom had acted during the Thanksgiving and Christmas holidays. There was a picture of Mom on Christmas Day that lingered in Margaret's mind. "She just looked vacant," Margaret said. We talked about what might be wrong with our mother: denial, depression, dementia, Alzheimer's disease. These were a few things that we discussed.

When we arrived home, Mom was glad to see me. It was one in the morning. We hugged and said our greetings. Mom, Margaret, and Norman cheerfully spoke. Margaret made mention of a necklace that Mom was wearing. We all spoke briefly. It was late. Margaret and Norman went to Jackson, a town thirty minutes away: Mom and I went to bed.

As I undressed in the room where my father took his last breath, I wondered what these next few days would be like for me. I looked around and missed Dad's physical presence in the home. I thought that Mom and I could go visit her sister, Anna Lee. Maybe we could go shopping at Wal-Mart or go visit some of her old friends. I wanted this time to be a time of change for Mom. She had gone through the worst few months of her life, and this could be a time to get a new focus. I had big ideas for us, how to spend two days—a time to celebrate her newfound freedom. Mom had given her entire life to others. This was the time for her. Mom's sons and daughters were all successful, and we could spend some time and some money to spoil her. I was willing to be a grand chauffeur, if needed. But little did I know, Mom was going to need more than I could give her.

The next morning we got up early for a new day. Mom cooked breakfast, as usual when I would visit home. We sat and talked a little while. Things seemed to be all right. Mom ate a little breakfast, then headed back to bed. I thought she was just tired from getting up to let us in at one o'clock in the morning, so I finished my breakfast and started my day. My high hopes were beginning to dwindle about spending time with Mom. As the day went on, she continued to lie in bed. I knew something was wrong, but did not know what. Mom was not the mom I knew. She wasn't Mom grieving, she was a different person. I kept myself busy during the day and called my sisters to see if this was how Mom had been acting. They confirmed the behavior, but did not know how much Mom had been sleeping throughout the day. I started to keep a journal of the day's events. We made it through the day, but I was highly disappointed.

I had made a few calls to my wife and children. I wanted to get support from Sara to see if I was thinking right. I thought that maybe Mom was suffering from severe depression. How could I get someone who has been so independent all her life to seek counseling? I knew that just the thought of this would make her mad. As I settled in for the evening, Mom asked me to go to the store and get her some laxatives. She wanted sodium citrate. I knew what this medicine would do to her digestive system, since I had had a lower G.I. examination performed the prior year. This medicine had one purpose: to clean you out. Mom had not had enough food that day to warrant taking this medicine. I told her that I would not get it for her. This started a definite behavior change. Mom had been sleeping most of the day. After I told her no, she started going to the bathroom a lot. She would walk from her bedroom to the bathroom. She would moan, and talk under her breath. As I observed this, I noticed that it was getting progressively worse. Mom was not actually going to the bathroom, just going back and forth. It appeared that she was playacting. She was serious. The highlight of this episode was when she came into the living room where I was sitting. She yelled at me, "If I die, this will be on your head." I explained to Mom that I knew what that medicine would do to her. She snapped and said, "How would you know?" I told her about my lower G.I. procedure. She replied, "Oh." I felt as if I were being conned, manipulated, controlled. I was at the point where I thought I needed to leave. What was going on inside her head? I called Brenda.

Brenda had taken the lead role with Mom for many years. She would travel twice per month to check on her. She would pay her bills, balance her checkbook, drive her to appointments, and do anything Mom needed. I called with the hopes that she could calm Mom down. Brenda explained that it was the same thing that precipitated her behavior at her home during the holidays. I handed the phone to Mom. Brenda talked to her a little while, with Mom getting worse while talking. I was starting to fear that Mom would become violent. When Brenda and Mom finished their conversation, Mom threw the phone at me. "Brenda wants to talk to you," she said. I felt as if I had lost the war with Mom. Brenda told me to just get the laxative for her, and that she would be down in two days for Mom's doctor appointment. She assured me that she would cover this with Mom.

I went to Wal-Mart and bought the sodium citrate for Mom. I felt as if I were buying contraband for a junkie. I came home and gave her the bottle. I told Mom the only reason I said no was because this medicine was not good for her. I explained that she had not eaten much at all that day and if she took the medicine, it was going to deplete any chance of her getting nutrients that day.

I said my peace and went to my bedroom. I sat their a while and wondered what was going on with Mom. I started to chronicle Mom's day on my laptop; I thought it would be beneficial when Brenda took Mom to the doctor.

Chronicle: January 7, 2004
Observation of Georgia Taylor:

I, Coleman Taylor, am writing this to help with trying to get my mother some help. Mom's husband died seven weeks ago, and I am concerned about her physical, mental, and emotional health. I arrived at Mom's house at one A.M. on January 7, 2004. Mom seemed happy to see me. We talked for a few minutes, and both went to bed.

7:00, I got up from bed.

8:00, Mom got up from bed, she cooked scrambled eggs for me. She had a few bites of cereal and a four-ounce glass of orange juice. She had prepared two slices of bacon, but did not eat it, gave to me.

8:45, she tried to call her sister on the telephone. She was unable to recall the number. She found her number on a piece of paper, but was not able to dial the number. She tried several times, with no success. I dialed the number, and she talked for three to five minutes. She did not end her conversation, just put the phone down, resulting in the phone making a beeping sound. I hung up the phone. During our conversation at the breakfast table, Mom stated that she had lost her necklace. When my sister Margaret dropped me off at Mom's house, she noticed the necklace Mom was wearing. At breakfast, Mom had stated that she lost her necklace and thought that Margaret had broken it last night, when she commented on the necklace, that was on Mom's neck.

8:55, Mom complained that she was tired and needed to lie down. She did. While Mom napped, I called Margaret and told her about the comment made by Mom and that mom was getting back into bed. I typed a letter for Mom, noting that she needed an attorney to draw up some papers. I took a shower and got ready for the day.

10:15, Mom got up and said she felt better; she had needed that rest. She asked me to pay her house payment for her. She gave me the information, and I wrote the check. She started to sign the check, but wasn't sure how to complete spelling her name. I assisted her by telling her the next letter of her name. Mom went on a hunt for the return envelope for her payment. After talking with my sister Brenda later that day, I found out there was no return envelope for her payment. Mom looked around for about ten minutes, and then produced a white envelope. "Mom, don't worry about that; I can pick up some envelopes at Wal-Mart. I have to go and get some ink for my printer." She still searched, until she found a plain envelope.

Mom laid seven dollars on the table and told me to buy her a stamp. I bought a book of twenty stamps for her. I returned around eleven A.M.; Mom was in bed.

11:00, Mom said she was cold. I raised the temperature for her while she stayed in bed.

11:30, I printed the letter to the attorney and got her papers together. I placed her payment in the mailbox to be picked up. At this point, I was updating Mom on everything that I was doing. It appeared to me that she had a lack of trust of the people around her, so I would let her know what I was doing. After printing the letter to the attorney, I read it to her. She liked it. She was still in bed.

11:40, I left the house to meet with Frankie Stanfill, Esq.

12:15, I returned home, and Mom was still in bed. I asked if she was okay and she stated that she was cold. I told her that she needed to eat, because she had not eaten much that morning. She asked me to microwave her a sweet potato; I did. She ate about half of it, along with some orange juice. She stated that she was starting to feel better. I wanted to get Mom out of the house; she had been in bed most of the morning. I asked if she wanted to go to her sister's, so she could get out and see people. She said she didn't feel good enough to go out in this weather. If the car broke down, then she would be stuck out in the cold and would get sick.

After eating, Mom went to the living room and we talked for a little while, approximately twenty minutes. We talked about grief and how we both had handled Dad's passing away. I stated that I was going to the grave site later in the day and asked if Mom wanted to go. She said it was too cold for her to go out.

12:45, Mom went to the kitchen and was looking for something. I walked in to see that she was getting her medicines out to take some. There are six bottles (two Zetia, two Protonix, one Zocor, and one Furosemide). She took one Protonix.

12:50, she was back in bed.

1:00, I went to my Dad's grave site.

1:15, I went to my rental property and visited with my tenant.

2:00, returned home; Mom was still in bed.

2:15–3:00, I took a nap in the TV room; Mom was still in bed.

3:00, put in video of my daughter's Christmas play to see if Mom would get up and watch it.

3:10, Mom came to the TV room to watch the video.

3:12, R.J. and Malik came to visit (Mom's grandson and great-grandson) .

3:14, Mom went to bed again.

4:00, R.J. and Malik left.

4:00–6:00, Mom remained in bed and requested that I both turn up the heat and cut down the heat.

6:00, I told Mom I was going to Sonic. I asked if she needed anything; she wanted a shake. I asked what kind, but she did not know. Vanilla? No. Chocolate? No. Strawberry? No. She tried to explain to me what kind she wanted, but could not give me a clue. I told her I would bring her a shake. I brought her a vanilla shake. She told me to put it in the refrigerator. I did.

7:30, Mom asked me to bring her the milkshake. I did. She drank just a little of it. She was still in her bed.

7:45, Mom came to the TV room and watched some TV—five minutes. She went to the kitchen and drank approximately six ounces of magnesium citrate. She came back to the TV room and asked if I would go to Wal-Mart to get her some more of the magnesium citrate. I told her no, because I was concerned that she had not eaten enough and that this stuff would not be good for her to take. She went back to her room again. She made frequent trips to the bathroom.

8:00–9:00, Mom started to moan and complain that she could not go to the bathroom and really needed the magnesium citrate. She had a very scared look on her face.

8:30, Mom said that she hoped that I was comfortable with my decision and that if she died, it would be on me. I told her that if she was not eating enough, and cleaning herself out with the medicine, she was not giving her body a chance to get fed.

8:45, called my sister Brenda and told her what was going on. Brenda stated that Mom had done the same thing two weeks ago, when she stayed at her house after Christmas. I asked Mom if she wanted to talk to Brenda; she said yes. She was coming out of the bathroom and came to the living room. She was very loud and had a look of distress on her face. She was very emotional when she talked to Brenda. She made statements that I was laughing at her and she just needed that magnesium citrate. At this point, she was crying and was angry with me. Brenda asked to speak with me. Brenda advised me to just get the medicine, because if I did not, Mom would only get worse emotionally.

9:00, I went to Wal-Mart.

9:30, I gave Mom the magnesium citrate. She drank four ounces.

10:00, I went to bed; Mom was already in bed. I did not hear her during the night.

General Observations: Mom keeps cutting the central air on and off. Justification for forgetting things: everybody forgets things. Could not remember names of children, or frequent phone numbers, such as her sister's. Forgetting to take medications. Not knowing how to spell her first and last name. A fear that someone was doing something to her (Margaret must have broken her necklace; "I know she didn't mean to ... but I can't find my necklace").

Mom did not get out of her nightclothes on January 7, 2004; did not take hair down from bobby pins; did not take a bath; did not eat enough to keep healthy: four to five bites of cereal; four ounces of juice; one-half sweet potato; one cup of coffee; four to five sips of vanilla shake.

Was in bed or asleep twelve out of fourteen hours on January 7, 2004.

8:00–10:00, January 7, 2004, emotional outbreak when denied magnesium citrate; crying; moaning; hypersensitive or paranoid.

I have written this chronicle so that it might give some insight into how Mom lives day to day. I know she is a caring and wonderful person. I believe there is either a chemical imbalance or a mental health issue that needs to be diagnosed, or perhaps a general nutrient issue that is causing this behavior change. I don't feel comfortable with Mom living by herself and have offered to bring her to live with my family. I have suggested that she should consider staying with someone a while to help get her into a routine.

This letter is written with love and for the love of my mother. She is loved and respected by all of her children and family. We want Mom to be able to live a happy and productive life.

Respectfully submitted,
Coleman Taylor
January 8, 2004

My two days of getting Mom out of her depression were a horrible failure. I had packed my bags, had breakfast, and was waiting for Margaret. She was going to take me to the Nashville Airport. I had completed my chronicle of Mom's first day. I had a copy ready for Margaret and Brenda. Brenda would be dropping by soon to pick up Mom. The two sisters came at different times. Margaret arrived first, and a few minutes later, Brenda arrived. I gave them a copy of the chronicle so that they could see what it was like staying here with Mom. This was the first time just one person had stayed with Mom since Dad's death. They were surprised to see how much Mom stayed in bed. They both commented that when they would call Mom, she would answer the phone, but did not know that she was lying in bed talking. I also made a copy for the doctor. I asked Brenda to make sure the doctor got a copy of my chronicle. I thought it would give a clear insight as to the root cause of Mom's emotional problem. Margaret and I took off for Nashville. Brenda stayed to take Mom to the doctor.

I made it back to Orlando without a hitch. My family was there to greet me outside the luggage pickup. After we made it back home, Mom called me. I was in shock. I had watched her fumble the phone just days before. She could not remember her sister's phone number, a number that had been the same for thirty years. How could she call me? Mom apologized for her behavior. She said she knew there was something wrong when she started arguing with me. I told her I just wanted her to be healthy. We said our I love yous and goodbyes.

I later called Brenda to see what was going on. Brenda gave me the doctor's report: Mom was diagnosed with severe depression. The doctor also ordered more tests for Mom. They were to return in a couple of weeks for a follow-up visit. The doctor gave Mom a prescription for depression. Mom agreed to stay with Brenda for a couple of weeks. This would give her a chance to be around other people and Brenda a chance to monitor Mom.

During Mom's stay with Brenda, there was some more bad news. Mom's brother-in-law died. I found out about this and could not believe it. I made arrangements and flew back to Tennessee. It was going to be a fast thirty-six-hour trip. There was a company meeting in Kansas City that I needed to attend. I made the trip to Nashville and rented a car. I drove to Jackson and spent the night with my sister Margaret. We spent a few waking moments together, then headed to bed. The next morning, we had breakfast at seven-thirty. My sister gave me a present, a CD by Luther Vandross. There was a song about his father passing, "Dance with

My Father." On my way to my sister Brenda's house, I listened to the song and cried. The songs is about when he was young and the great memories of his childhood with his father. This lay heavy on my mind as I drove. I had missed my dad since his death. There were so many things I wanted to say to him. So I spoke out loud in the car and talked to him. I told him how I missed him and that I would look after Mom.

Brenda lived seventy miles from Margaret. I made the drive with great anticipation. Mom did not know that I was coming in for a short visit. I could only spend about three hours with her before going to my uncle's viewing. Then, after the viewing, I had to drive back to Nashville, to fly back to Orlando. The next day I was flying to Kansas City for the year-beginning meeting. I drove to my sister's house, got out of the car, and knocked on the door; my sister answered. We hugged, and I asked if Mom knew that I was coming. She said no. She had told her that Jerry, my sister's husband, had a friend coming over. As I stood in the living room, Brenda called Mom to come and meet Jerry's friend. Mom came down the hallway and saw it was me. I gave her a hug and a kiss. She had a smile on her face. She reminded me of a shy schoolgirl on her first date. She knew that I would make it here if I was going to see my uncle. She had a joyous look on her face. This was so wonderful to see, considering the last time I saw her and the unusual episode she had. We talked on the couch and she kept looking at me with that schoolgirl grin. We had coffee and a Danish and just enjoyed each other's company.

Time passed in a pleasant way, but I had to get on the road to make my uncle's viewing. I drove an hour to the viewing and paid my respects to my uncle. My cousin Sheila was there and we talked about her dad. He was a farmer, factory worker, deacon, and all-around businessman. He sold his crop to the local people out of the back of his truck. He would drive on Saturdays and visit and make sales. He would have watermelon, peas, corn, and whatever was in harvest. He had a cotton field. When I was young, we used to pick cotton for him. It was a great experience. Sheila and I talked and shared for a little while. I stopped by Anna Lee's house, my uncle's wife, to see how she was doing. She appeared to be all right. The bed was still in place where her husband had passed away. I gave my condolences and visited for a short time, and then headed out to catch my plane.

The drive back to the airport was quiet. The thought of getting Mom back on course with medical treatment was exciting. Mom and her sister were both new widows. Maybe they could spend time together and support each other. Maybe they could be the therapy for each other. The two women had given their lives for their husbands proudly. They were great examples of showing dignity when their husbands died. They were great examples of *for better or for worse, in sickness and in health*. It was their time to have some rest from all the strain they had willfully been under. I could not wait to return to see them again, and I had not even left Tennessee yet. The old saying that old people do get old is true, and it does bring sickness and death. We will all face it one day.

Chapter Eleven
What Are You Going to Do When You Get Old?

MY MOM was diagnosed with early onset of Alzheimer's disease and deep depression. Alzheimer's is something that most old southerners would joke about. They would play with the name Alzheimer, describing old people. They would call this disease "old timers' disease." It was a joke when someone would forget something obvious, and someone would say, "Sounds like you are suffering from old timers' disease."

Recalling the conversation with one of my sisters, after mom's doctor appointment, it became very evident that this was not a joke. The doctor asked Mom to repeat three words after him: dog, apple, ball. Mom could not repeat them back to him in sequence. The doctor set up an MRI and follow-up appointment to discuss medication for the depression.

As the weeks went by, all the children telephoned Mom. You could tell that she was getting better with her medication. She spent time with her friends and went to church. She was volunteering at a clothing store set up by the Catholic church. This became her therapy and interaction with others. It seemed that Mom was bouncing back to herself again. During this time, I asked her if she would like to visit Florida and spend time with my family. She agreed. I started to work on a plan to get Mom to Orlando. As it turned out, we set a date surrounding Candy's graduation from dental school. This would be Mom's first doctor in the family. What a great accomplishment. Grandmother could not afford dirt; granddaughter was graduating as a doctor.

Lloyd and I flew to Lexington without our families this time. It was a short in-and-out trip for Candy's graduation and celebration. Lloyd and I flew into Memphis airport and drove to Mom's house. Mom greeted us at the front door. She looked good. She was thinner than usual, but over all, she seemed happy to see us. We sat and had a meal with her, as usual. We talked a little while, but I wanted to get out of the house. It was night time and pretty dark outside. I wanted to drive by the rental property to see if the tenant was still there. I asked Lloyd if he wanted to go, but he said no. I asked Mom if she wanted to ride along; she said yes. We got into Mom's car. It was a station wagon, about fifteen years old. It still runs, and she offered her car to drive. I always drive Mom's car when in Lexington. It is a way of honoring her. Even though I would have a nice rental car with all the bells and whistles, I would drive her car. It was a way of saying, I'm still your son, and what you gave and offered me when I lived under your roof is still good now. I got Mom's walker and placed it in the back seat and we drove to the trailer.

This is the same property she drove to for years to pick up Aunt Mer. As we drove, it was nice to see that her health had improved since I saw her in January. Mom did not seem like her old self, but she was better than the last time I had seen her. We talked about the people who lived along that road. Mom was confused on some of the names. I did not place much weight behind it. It was just good being with Mom and spending time together. We made it to the trailer; the tenant still lived there. We talked a little bit by the road-side and then headed back to town.

We made it back to town and drove around a bit. I was tired of sitting in one place from that day. I had worked, then hopped on a plane. I wanted to unwind a little before going back to Mom's for the night. We drove by her friend Lucille's house. Lucille was sitting on her front porch. It was late May and the weather felt great outside. I pulled up and Lucille said, "I thought that was Georgia's car."

We pulled up and had a chat by the car. When I visit Mom, I always try to see people who made an impact on my life. Mrs. Teen was going to spend the night at Lucille's because of the forecast of thunderstorms later that night. As we were talking, Mrs. Teen joined us. We had a good laugh and talked for a while. I told them that I was writing a book about old people, and I asked if I could take some pictures of them the next day. They agreed. Mom and I said our goodbyes and headed home. Mom's spirits were lifted after seeing her friends. We met back up with Lloyd at her house and set-tled in for the night.

When morning came, the phone rang. It was Lucille, asking when I was coming by to take pictures. I told them to give me thirty minutes and I would be there. I made the appointment and drove by myself. When I arrived, I was surprised. Lucille and Mrs. Teen were dressed, with full makeup, ready for their glamour shots. I went in and took some pictures. I sat down for a while and they told me that they needed to tell me something. I was open and ready to hear what they had to say.

They spoke of an incident earlier that month. Mom had driven all three of them to the homecoming at Timberlake Grove Church. The experience was scary because of Mom's declining driving skills. They voiced their concerns and told me that they wanted to let Mom know that they would not be riding with her anymore. They did not think she should be driving. This was a major concern for me also. I had thought about this and wondered if Mom could get around without a car. This would be a blow to her if she could not drive. She had always been the one to get behind the wheel of a car and go anywhere. I knew that she was going to be in Florida for two weeks. This would give me a chance to talk to Brenda to relay the information to her for the next doctor visit. I thanked them and headed back to Mom's house. There, we had breakfast and started getting ready for the big event for the day.

We made the trip to the Memphis Coliseum, uneventfully. We brought along a wheelchair so that Mom would not have to do much walking. We made it into the event, and Mom looked lost. She was aware that Candy was graduating, but did not really want to be in a crowd. After the graduation, we met Candy outside, wearing her cap and gown, to take pictures. Mom mentioned how proud she was of Candy. After a few pictures, she was ready to go. As we drove home, Mom got carsick. This was something I had never experienced with her. We stopped and bought some crackers and water. She had some, and it seemed to settle her stomach.

At the celebration, at Margaret's house, we were together again as a family. Al could not make it to the celebration because of both work and the long drive. We were happy to see Candy graduate, and this gathering also gave the sisters and brothers a chance to check on Mom. She was very anxious at the celebration, and after about an hour, she was ready to get back to her home. We stayed for a few hours and then finally returned Mom to her home. She was worn out, but made some very favorable comments about Candy's accomplishments.

The next day was the big day. Mom was going to come to Orlando and visit for two weeks with Lloyd and me. We stayed up late and made sure we had Mom packed for the trip. The night was uneventful and we made the flight reservation from Memphis to Orlando without a hitch. Mom stayed with Lloyd for the first week and with my family the second week. While staying with us, we had Mom on her medication daily. Her ability to interact with the family was good. I could tell that the children would get on her nerves some. She tried to make efforts to show interest in their homework and ask questions about what happened during their day.

During Mom's stay we made memories. I thought that if the disease got worse, this time with Mom might be the best it gets. This could be a moment in time that I would look back at and the children would say, "I remember that time when Grandmama did this or that." My schedule with Mom was going to be full also. My brother Al was in Orlando, in from Ohio, and we spent time with his family. This was the beginning of the summer break from school and one of the busiest travel times of the year, especially for Orlando. Margaret was to fly in this week to Orlando for a conference. She was going to fly back to Memphis with Mom at the end of the week.

At this point in my career, I had obtained some success. I was proud to show Mom my new house. It had a screened-in pool; this was something I had only dreamed of while growing up. We had plenty of space, and I wanted her to see what a great impact she had made on my life. Mom always took great pride in our accomplishments. For her, the things her children were doing were something she never thought would come true, not in her lifetime.

Sara and I gave Mom the master bedroom during her stay. This would give her privacy and her space to rest when she wanted. Since Mom's unfortunate event in the fifties left her semi-paralyzed, she has had an issue with incontinence. This would give her a private bathroom to accommodate her needs.

Mom went to church with us on Sunday. After church we came home and had lunch, and the children and I played in the pool. We planned to visit Sea World the next day, after I finished work. We made our way to Sea World. We had about six hours to catch the show and have a bite to eat. We made it through to the big finale: Shamu Rocks America. This was a hit. Mom saw the large whales jumping in the air, bringing a great smile to her face. At the end of the show they send the whales out to spray the crowd. While we were watching the show, it started to thunder and lightning. I looked at the lightning strikes across the sky to see if we were in any danger. I looked at Mom and she was about five feet behind me. We were halfway up the stadium, but she thought the whales were going to spray her. She had a childlike smile on her face and giggled like a little girl. This made me smile and it perplexed me about the drastic reaction. I wanted to just enjoy the moment. As the show ended, the thunderstorm blew in on us. Mom, Sara, and our four children made the mad dash to the car. We were at the back of the park; this was going to be a long haul. Lightning and thunder surrounded us as we ran. I was pushing Mom in her wheelchair and Sara pushed the stroller with our two youngest children. The two older children had umbrellas and tried to stay dry. They were unsuccessful. The water was cold and the thunder was loud. The lightning was fearful. We pushed on with our dash to the finish line—the parking lot—laughing the whole way. As we made it across the park, Mom's laughter was so warm and true. The party of seven was having a great time in the moment, making unexpected memories. We all made it to the car okay. We turned on the heat in the car. It was June and the heat was on in the car in Florida? Hmm.

A few days later was Mom's birthday. We had the honor of having Mom on her birthday at our home. Sara and I wanted to make it special for her. We ordered her a cake from the bakery and made reservations to see Cirque du Soleil, to entertain Mom. We thought this would give the children a new experience to share with their grandmother, to make memories. The show was great, and Mom seemed to enjoy it also. We headed back home after the show to eat cake and ice cream.

Mom's actions during the day were suspect. It seemed that she was uncomfortable. I watched her actions to evaluate what we could do to help her. She said she was fine and thanked us for the presents and festivities.

As the night came to a close, I asked Sara about Mom's day. Sara said that Mom was more distant. She didn't know if Mom was expecting a huge party, or missing Dad, or what. So we just maintained a level of service to her. We were in a position to take care of Mom if she needed anything. She was just having a down day.

Mom wrapped up her stay in Orlando. Margaret had flown in for a conference, and then the two of them traveled back to Tennessee together.

As usual, I called to see how things had gone on the plane. Margaret said Mom's behavior was somewhat odd. Mom felt as if she could not eat on the plane. Margaret thought that Mom believed she had to pay for her lunch, or was just confused about the whole transaction. She stated that Mom was tired from the trip, but was in good spirits.

As time would pass, I would call Mom from time to time. The typical conversation would be, "Hey, what are you doing?" Mom would respond," I'm just laying here in bed. I'm not feeling well." This became her hideout from the world. This would also speed up her rapid decline in health.

Brenda continued to travel twice per month, or however many times Mom needed her help. She was the one who would take Mom to her appointments. The appointment after her visit did not go well. The doctor did not want her to drive. He ordered a driving test to be given to Mom. They made the appointment for a few weeks later. Mom and Brenda kept the appointment at the driving test site. Mom took the test and failed the written part. She took the driving part of the test. An instructor rode along with her and graded how she performed. Mom failed this part also. This was a blow to her. It could also be a blessing. The thought of Mom hurting herself was a horrible thought. Even worse was the thought of Mom hurting someone else while driving.

Mom took the news hard. How could she get to the store and go where she needed to go? This was her main concern. Knowing Mom, I knew she would not take this sitting down. She went home upset, but still drove around when she needed to. She made trips to the store and to see friends. I called her one day to see how the loss of her driver's license affected her. She told me that she had to do what she needed to do to get food and supplies. One part of me understood, the other part of me did not.

As Mom and I talked, I wanted to somehow let her know that what she was doing was wrong. Over the phone was not the right time to do this, so I wrote her a letter. I asked her to consider the possibility of staying with one of her children. I tried to share the family's concerns about her being by herself. I sent the letter. I also talked to Mom that night. I told her that I had sent her a letter and wanted her to consider what I had written.

A few days later she received the letter and I called to get her response. She was not offended, but said she felt that I was writing out of love for her. As the summer days grew to an end, Mom's condition grew worse. Each phone call was sluggish. She would have good moments and bad moments. She would ask how many children I had. She would ask if I had any boys. These questions alone were hard. Mom knew just a few months ago how many children I had and that they were all girls. She would be in bed as we talked. I would get her version of what was going on in the world. Her world was becoming her home. She was growing paranoid.

Once, when RJ, her grandson, was on leave from the navy, he paid Mom a visit. He went by Mom's house; he knocked on the door, but no one answered. Mom was inside the house. She did not recognize him, so she did not open the door. Just a few months before, Mom would have known him. She would have had a large dinner fixed for RJ. She would have enjoyed his company. When this episode happened, I realized that Mom was losing memories, and this was the way it was going to be.

There were events that took place in 2004 regarding Mom's health that, as a son, I will not share. They are horrible and should be kept private. This disease, Alzheimer's, was stealing my Mom's memories, and was slowly killing her children's memories. The horrible thing is that in the early stages of this disease, the person who has it does know they have it. If they know they have it, they might not accept that they have it and ignore the signs of the disease. They can still function at a high level, like cooking, driving, shopping, and working daily chores. The loss of certain memories leaves you to think that this person is not the same person. How could Mom still do all this stuff and forget my name? At a certain point visiting with Mom, I thought that maybe she was acting. This could not be real. I kept waiting for the punchline, or someone to say, "Fooled you." This never happened.

Mom's way of dealing with the apparent loss of certain memories was to blame it on her age. "I just can't remember certain things like I used to; I'm just getting old," she would say. The truth is, she was getting older, and so were the rest of us. The strain of dealing with disease placed a lot of stress on the siblings. We wanted to do what was right for Mom. The word "right" is a hard word to describe to a person with Alzheimer's disease. Mom thought she could function as normal. She could not. Basic housecleaning was poor. Mom's hygiene was less than before. Mom's definition of right was not the same as her children's definition of right. The family tried to keep her dignity in place and prepare for the worst of this disease. We are still coping with the dichotomy of how to help someone when they don't want your help.

The loss of my dad and my mom's bout with Alzheimer's disease has changed my life forever. It has challenged my own mortality. What is the advantage of getting old? What do we have to look forward to in life? What was the purpose of going through life and fighting battles only to surrender to the things that old age has to offer: pain, heartache, disease, and loneliness? Alzheimer's disease is a thief. I must fight it with all I have. I must keep my mom's memories alive. I must honor her by doing what's right, by being there for her when she needs me. I must be able to see the person through the disease, to separate the disease from the person.

The gift of long life is to share it with others as you live. The passing on of sayings and sharing of wisdom is a way for people to share their experiences in life: the joy of seeing a young boy's eyes light up when someone gives him his first baseball; the kitchen talks that change a young person's life from making horrible mistakes to taking a turn for the best. The traditions of doing what is right and living a good life are the benefits. The choice of leaving a legacy on this earth, a chance to see the seeds planted by an old person and getting a chance to see them grow: This is the beauty of old people.

As the baby boomers get older, the disease of Alzheimer's is more prevalent. In years past, this disease was considered as senility of the old; however, this disease is a thief that takes families unaware. Warriors who fought in wars, even Ronald Reagan, the president of the United States, have fallen to this mighty enemy. When we look in the mirror and face the truth, we are getting older, day by day. The reflection does not reveal the question, or the answer: What are you going to do when you get old?

Reflections

AS THE Taylor family deals with the uncertainty of Alzheimer's disease, we are faced with many hard decisions. Can we honor our mom as she has honored so many in their lives? Can we be there when she needs us? Can we keep up with this terrible change in her behavior and still be at peace with Mom? We can only answer these questions as time goes by. All the siblings have the same desire to do what's right for Mom. We are all hurting on different levels. A mom's love touches each child uniquely. So goes our pain with Mom. *Love conquers all* is an old saying. Can it help us conquer this horrible disease?

I have searched the Web, watched videos, and read information about how to deal with aging and disease. There is a tough road ahead for all of us, including Mom. The only thing I know is that the example set by Mom is one that is hard to match. She always said that we did not have much money, but we were rich in love. Mom loved everyone. Now it is our turn to show her that the love she gave did not go in vain.

We love you, Mom, and wish only the best for you. You are a wonderful person and a special gift from God to all your children. How fortunate we are to have you as our mom.

Mom, I know that Dad has passed to another world and is in a better place. I ask myself daily, "What would Dad want me to do for you?" The answer is to love you. I do love you, and want to make your life a pleasure, just as you did for me. I am eternally grateful for you. May God bless and keep you.

Your son,
Coleman